Full Series

Rock
your
Moxie

Power Moves for Women
Leading the Way

5 Secrets *of*
Women Who Have
Made It to the Top

5 Strategies *for*
Warp Speed Growth

5 Beliefs *of*
Winning Women

5 Ways
Influential Women
Sustain Their Edge

5 Habits *of*
Ridiculously
Successful Women

*Special
Edition*

by Maureen Berkner Boyt

Maureen's insights have powerful paybacks. She not only knows how women succeed; she equips you to do it for yourself.
--Debra Benton, author *The CEO Difference: How to Climb, Crawl, and Leap Your Way to the Next Level of Your Career*

This series helps women to discover the most important truth in advancing their leadership: You are the most powerful change agent in your own journey. A must read for anyone committed to unleashing the ingenuity and talent of half our population in order to create innovative solutions for *all* of us.
--Tiffany Dufu, Chief Learning Officer, Levo League

Do you want to talk about growth or do you want to grow? If you want to grow, start here. Accessible and practical, Maureen Berkner Boyt's books give you advice that will propel you straight out of your comfort zone into a whole new world. Just do it!
--Jodi Detjen, Suffolk University Professor and co-author, *The Orange Line: A Woman's Guide to Integrating Career, Family and Life*

Make no mistake—mentors do matter. When you need real world advice to gain and retain your seat at the leadership table, look no further. This highly readable book series stands in as your personal sponsor, showing you actionable steps and providing that pat on the back and gentle shove forward we all need from time to time. So, *Rock Your Moxie* --take action, take risk, and take charge.

--Connie Duckworth, Founder/CEO, ARZU STUDIO HOPE and author of *The Old Girls' Network: Insider Advice to Women Building Businesses in a Man's World*

Finally a book series for women that connects all the dots! Whether you're a senior executive or emerging leader, Maureen's Power Moves will get you in winning shape and stretching beyond boundaries.

--Linda Bernier, Senior Vice President, Trizetto Corporation

Maureen's core message—"Get off your tush and do it!"-- is energizing and her moxie is contagious. Readers will inhale the books and race to start implementing Maureen's sensible and concrete leadership advice.

--Meg Cadoux Hirshberg, author, *For Better or For Work: A Survival Guide for Entrepreneurs and Their Families*

Maureen Berkner Boyt is refreshingly candid, insightful, and even a bit edgy as she delivers real world advice and strategies all women can use. Made for any woman wanting to achieve more or be more, this series is a guidebook for making it happen.

--Alison Martin-Books, CEO of Mentoring Women's Network, Author of *"Landing on My Feet: Learning to Lead Through Mentoring"*

Maureen Berkner Boyt has a winner here for women who are focused on succeeding in big ways - for themselves, their companies, communities and the world. Her *Rock Your Moxie* series enables women to take their place at any table - business, government, world tables - at a time when women's voices are so sorely needed.

--Barbara Osterman, Founder and President, Human Solutions LLC

Maureen Berkner Boyt is a high performance leader who shares her top notch formula for women to win in the new world of work. In her Rock Your Moxie series, she focuses on straight talk and best practices that elevate effectiveness that takes women to the next level. Whether you're on the corporate ladder or building your own business, the insights and information in this series is relevant, actionable and just what women leaders need to hear right now.

--Lisa Hendrickson, President, Spark City

Maureen Berkner Boyt has put together a series of invaluable knowledge and insights that help women rise to their potential and harness their strengths. Maureen's books on leadership are an invaluable resource and must have in this ever changing, hyper speed world. I will be keeping mine at arms reach on my desk so that I can refer to them daily.

--Tamara Kleinberg, serial entrepreneur & founder of
TheShuuk.com

Rock Your Moxie is for women leaders who are already committed to playing big. If this isn't your first rodeo and you're looking for a way to seriously step up your game, then you just picked up a game changer. In this series, Maureen Berkner Boyt brilliantly provides chapter after chapter of meaningful clarity and guidance garnered from lessons learned in the trenches. Full of breakthrough takeaways and tangible tools, be prepared to rock your world.

--Kris Boesch, Founder & CEO, Choose People

This series is dedicated to my tribe, the women of the world who are committed to growth, leading the way and making a difference.

Keep rocking your moxie!

Table of Contents

Preface

———————

You are not alone. You picked up this book because you are a successful woman who wants *more*. You are want to be more, have a bigger impact, make more money, and call bigger and bigger shots. I wrote this series to help you accelerate that process and to help catapult you forward from wherever you are today. Success and leadership are not rocket science, but they require thinking the right way and doing the right things, consistently.

I've done the research for you. I've spent the past few years interviewing some of the brightest, most dynamic, successful women in the business world. I've also traveled the country visiting local chapters of The Moxie Exchange Movement and engaging in meaningful business and leadership conversations with professional women who are investing in their own learning and growth. I've spent hundreds of hours around rock star female leaders discussing and dissecting leadership and success for women. I've paid attention, watched for patterns, taken notes, and distilled the ideas here – for you. I'm sharing what I've learned in this book and in the *Rock Your Moxie* series.

Each book covers five ideas with five coinciding Power Moves that will propel you forward. The books are designed to be short, powerful and pack a punch. Think of reading them as being akin to participating in a full-body contact sport rather than being a spectator at that same game. Growing personally and as a leader is work. It requires that you get off the sidelines, take off your protective gear, and get in there and play to your full potential. I know you are up to the challenge. I suggest you read a chapter at a time, digest the information, and take action on the ideas that really resonate with you.

I'll refer to the knowing/doing gap throughout the books. That's the place where average performers live. It's the gap between saying, 'Well of *course* I should do that. Everybody knows *that*.' to actually getting off your tush and doing it. Crossing the gap means making the changes and implementing the ideas and thinking that high performing women use everyday. Be thinking about how the ideas apply to you, be honest in your assessment of where you stand and move forward toward being a better leader and more successful version of who you are today.

I want you to succeed in a ridiculously big way. I want that for you individually and for us collectively as women. So, I don't pull any punches and I'm not blowing smoke up anyone's skirt in the books. There are bigger issues at play here. It's time to change the face of leadership in the business world. This last decade was supposed to be the time when women made gains that brought us close to parity in the boardroom and executive suite, and instead the needle has barely moved. That gets me wrapped around the axle. Why? Long ago power was held in the church, more in recently government and now it rests in the business world. If we're going to make a positive difference in the world, we need women at the table.

We need YOU at the table.

If you really want to make the abysmal stats about male/female ratios in leadership positions come to life, spend some time on the 'Executive Team' and 'Leadership Team' pages of mid to large sized companies. If you're prone to high blood pressure, I don't recommend this activity for you. It is truly appalling- page after page of middle-aged white guys in various colored ties and stages of male pattern baldness peppered by the occasional woman.

I swear I've gone through four of the five stages of grief in this process: denial, anger, bargaining, and depression. But, HELL NO, I am not landing on the last stage of 'acceptance'!

Let me be clear that I have nothing against middle-aged white guys. I'm married to a spectacular one, we need men in leadership positions, and this isn't about 'us vs. them' and victimization. It is about how we move the dial on the numbers. It's about making the numbers 'real' for decision makers. It's about stepping up and owning your own abilities and throwing your name in the hat when opportunities arise. It's about finding mentors and sponsors to propel your career, and being the same to women coming up behind you. Whatever you do, don't 'accept' that this is the way things have been and will always be in the business world.

When things are terrible, people get fired up and start making changes. When things are 'good enough' complacency sets in. In the business world, things are 'good enough' for women right now. There are enough opportunities in middle management that the lack of women in the C-suite isn't causing an uproar. The days of butt-pinching machismo are for the most part a distant memory. In fact men and women are getting along just swimmingly, so the fact that women are only making 77% of what men earn is barely causing a yawn. Women no longer have to bring their husbands along to co-sign for a business loan (which was happening as recently as the late 80's) so the fact that they rarely have access to the big money (1 million plus loans, venture and angel dollars) doesn't cause a stir.

Things are just good enough that they are killing us in terms of forward progress. The dial on critical factors (pay, executive positions, board of directors' seats, elected office...) has barely moved in the past 15 years. It's a sad state of affairs. And guess what? It impacts YOU.

What to do? Step up, step out and move the dial. If things are going to change collectively, as women we need to grow individually. That starts with you committing to your own growth as you read this book. That takes me back to wanting you to be ridiculously successful for you and for "us".

On the issue and impact of the dearth of women leaders in business, we've got to change the numbers, and that means taking action. Roll up your sleeves, and create a plan as you read. Really use the Power Moves section at the end of each chapter to help guide your planning and ensuing action. By the end of the series you should have a rock-solid, kick butt, get-after-it plan for success and owning your place at the next summit in your leadership journey. I look forward to hearing your stories of success, leadership and how you're getting after it in a big way! Send me an *email mo@moxieexchange.com* or join the conversation and community on my blog *www.moxieexchange.com/blog* Rock your moxie!

Maureen Berkner Boyt

Javea, Spain / Fort Collins, Colorado

Nº1

Rock your Moxie

Power Moves for Women Leading the Way

5 Secrets *of* **Women Who Have Made It to the Top**

by Maureen Berkner Boyt

Rock Your Moxie:

Power Moves for Women Leading the Way

5 Secrets of Women Who Have Made It To The Top

Maureen Berkner Boyt

Table of Contents

Click here to join a community of women in an online monthly workshop covering ideas and Power Moves from the book

Chapter 1: Own It and Create It

The advice in this chapter is going to be short and sweet. You've probably heard it before, however it IS game changing for most women when they fully embrace it. It is also one of those truths that seems to break open the largest knowing/doing gap (more like a Grand Canyon!) for average performers. High performing women who are leading the way have a profound understanding of the following principles and it has allowed them to soar. Their secret is that they live by these principles instead of just knowing about them.

They understand that if they know their own strengths and abilities and acknowledge those strengths and abilities, it's a leadership accelerator.

It's amazing to me how quickly we teach girls not to 'own it.' Last year at MoxieFest (a leadership and mentoring event for girls hosted by The Moxie Exchange Movement) I was sitting at a table with four teenaged girls ranging in age from 12-15. I asked them a simple question, "What are you good at?" The question, and the underlying ramifications, turned out not to be so simple. The girls could not answer the question. It truly stumped them.

After some prodding and encouragement from me, one of the girls brightly proclaimed, "I'm good at soccer!" I watched her face light up when the realization that she WAS good at something dawned on her. More prodding and encouragement from me had another of the girls come to the realization that she was, "pretty good at school." Not as much conviction, not as much excitement. Two of the girls were unable to respond. They could not come up with a single thing they thought they were good at. I even asked the question in a different way, "What would your MOM say you were good at?" Nothing. I wanted to cry.

I'll just go ahead and state the obvious- women are really rotten at standing in their greatness, at taking credit for their share of work accomplished, at acknowledging they have gifts and talents that add to this party we call business and life. How many times have you heard a colleague say, 'it was nothing' or 'really it was the team that pulled it off' or something along those lines? All the time. We've got to come up with a better answer when someone points out what we've done. How about, 'I worked very hard to make that happen and am stoked that it all came together'. Or try this one on for size, 'The _____(fill in the blank) was right in my wheelhouse and I'm glad I was able to use my strengths to make it happen.'

We need to acknowledge our accomplishments and

understand what we're good at so the people around us can do the same. And sometimes, horror of horrors, we need to START the conversation about our accomplishments and what we're good at instead of waiting for someone else to take the lead. If we don't, it's likely that no one else will, and the numbers at the top will stayed stacked in the XY chromosome camp. Don't be an idiot about it– thank others who were involved who really pulled their weight, be gracious AND own your success and talents.

Here's my throw down challenge. I want to hear what YOU are good at. Actually, I want to hear, unapologetically, what you kick a** at, what big and small things you've accomplished that you're proud of, and what YOU bring to the party. Bring it on! Oh, and bring a girl to the party. They need to see that it's not only ok, but also necessary to know your strengths and own your accomplishments.

The two girls at MoxieFest who didn't know, or didn't feel comfortable acknowledging what they were good at? I filled in the blanks for them and shared what I thought they were good at from what I'd observed over the several hours we'd spent together. When all else fails, have a sister's back!

Along with owning it, rock star women are not expecting anyone else to do the heavy lifting. They live by the cheesy, but very, very true motto 'if it's to be, it's up to me.'

They understand that nobody is going to create success for them.

This is not the norm in the United States anymore. Somehow we've become a society of people who think we should be successful just because we're breathing, or that we can order it up like a medium fry. Those women who live in just the opposite manner are the ones leading the way. Action is fundamental to their thinking and behavior. They understand that you must act on ideas that are presented to you. You have to ask for more money if you want it. Only YOU decide whether you're angry, sad, optimistic or exuberant. Only YOU decide what you're going to get off your tush and implement. Only YOU are in charge of your success and leadership abilities.

Nobody is going to do this for you, sister. The only one stopping you from starting a business, getting the promotion, landing the big donor is YOU. If you give up at the first 'no', you own that. If you let a crappy boss get the best of you, you own it. If you stay the course, do the work, have a 'get it done' attitude, you own it. If you've been somewhere that great ideas are shared, it's up to YOU to own what you've learned and TAKE ACTION on the ideas. Nobody is going to ride that horse for you.

If you need a little more incentive, read *'Kabul Beauty School'* by Deborah Rodriguez. The glimpse it gives you into the lives of the women in the Middle East will give you pause. These women, against seemingly insurmountable odds, daily degradation, violence against women and no legal rights STILL are taking action, owning their experience and changing their lives for the better. That's some serious moxie!

Chapter 1 Power Moves

1. Create a list of your strengths, abilities and successes. Keep it in a handy place in an easily updateable format. Review it and add to it quarterly.

2. Ask five people to share what they believe your professional and leadership strengths are. Do not ask your parents! You won't believe them, because you'll think they're inherently biased, which they should be. If they are not, you shouldn't want to know what they think anyway! The five should include a mix of people in your world, such as a boss/former boss, co-worker, employee or direct report, good friend and your partner. Write down their responses and add them to your own list.

3. Get a group of 5-6 kick butt professional women together. Let them know in advance that each of you will be sharing

things you are good at, strengths you have and recent accomplishments. Provide wine if it's slow going at first! Joking aside, make sure each of you can articulate in a strong way what you're good at. This practice will help you 'own it' in real-world scenarios.

4. Create three lists in relation to your work and professional development: things to start doing, stop doing and stay the course on. Pick one each week to take action on.

5. At the end of each day, review your calendar. What action do you need to take based on what happened in your day? No more than three things should make the cut, so make them worth your time and energy.

Chapter 2 Learn to Draft

Here's the skinny; although we need to create our own success, we also need some key people pulling us along in their draft. What's drafting? It's a concept that the women you look up to in the business world learned as they were making their way to the top. Here's a definition from the world of aerodynamics:

"Drafting or slipstreaming is a technique where two vehicles or other moving objects are caused to align in a close group reducing the overall effect of drag due to exploiting the lead object's slipstream. Especially when high speeds are involved, as in motor racing and cycling, drafting can significantly reduce the paceline's average energy expenditure required to maintain a certain speed and can also slightly reduce the energy expenditure of the lead vehicle or object.

You need someone who is already sitting where you want to be in the business world to be that lead "object" and reduce the drag of trying to move forward as a lone wolf. That takes a hell of a lot of energy. Men embrace this concept and do it as naturally as breathing. We're part of the way there as women, but are missing a key component: sponsors.

There are stats that show women have as many mentors as men do. We nurture the heck out of one another in these relationships. As a result, we end up being over-developed and under-promoted. What we don't have, and what is critical to our success, are sponsors. Sponsors are mentors on steroids. They use their influence, open doors, actively advocate for you and let you draft off their success to build yours. And research show that *men have 3-4 times more sponsors than women do.*

Research conducted by The Center for Work-Life Policy and written up in *Harvard Business Review* highlights the importance of the 'sponsorship effect'. Those men and women with sponsors ask for and get more pay and stretch assignments and are far happier with their rate of advancement. Having sponsors then is critical to changing the game for women in business, and we have significantly fewer of them than men do.

It's imperative that entrepreneurial women understand this concept applies to them as well. I've seen far too many female business owners stunt their potential because they were grinding it out in the trenches alone. You can make it work that way, but it's going to take a lot more effort and time than if you had some key sponsors in your community and industry opening doors and making introductions for you. Take a look around you at some of the business owners who started their gig at about the same time you did who have leap-frogged you in terms of business growth and leadership clout. When you really start paying attention, I am willing to bet you a nice bottle of Spanish wine that they have some key sponsors in the business community drafting for them.

It's game time. We need to get ourselves some sponsors! How do we do that? This is where things are simple but not easy. You first have to *believe* that having someone advocate for you, that having powerful sponsors grease the skids for you, is not a sign of weakness. Why don't you pause a moment for dramatic effect while that sinks in. This is a biggie, one of the biggest secrets of successful women, in fact. They get this, and actively seek out and nurture sponsorship relationships. If you can get over the unfounded fear of seeming weak or unqualified if someone is helping you, you've just released the brakes.

Now, on to how to get a sponsor or two in your corner. First, identify those senior leaders or local business influencers whom you know have acted as sponsors for others in the past. Build your street credibility with them. Be smart, resourceful and willing to learn. Have a track record that shows you are on the move up and serious about growing as a leader. Create a clear plan for your professional growth and progress professionally. Then show a little moxie and ASK. Remember, the guys are, and they are killing us in terms of pay, promotions and influence. ASK,

ASK, ASK (consider this being your mantra for the year, or maybe the next 10 years for that matter.)

On the flip side, if you're in a position to be a sponsor, do it! Pick a few women you believe in, sit them down and explain what a sponsorship relationship looks like. Ask for their goals in writing and for them to articulate their vision for their career or business. If you think she's on the right track, start advocating for her. Take some calculated risks, draft for her and watch her thrive.

Chapter 2 Power Moves

1. Identify the people in your life who have served as your mentors or sponsors in the past. Reach out to them and thank them, sharing specifics about how their involvement in your professional life helped you succeed. Everybody loves and deserves to know they've had a positive impact!

2. Get over yourself. If you try and do it all solo, you're slowing down your growth and the potential impact you can have on the world. Get comfortable with the idea of having sponsors.

3. Pay attention and recognize the sponsorship relationships that are happening all around you. Who is involved? How

do the mechanics seem to work in your company, community and/or industry? Get familiar with the 'cultural norms' of sponsorship relationships in your particular corner of the world so you know how to play well in that sandbox.

4. Identify 3-4 people in your organization, community or industry who are 2-3 steps ahead of where you are. They should be sitting in a place where you want to go and be someone you admire.

5. Ask. Sets up meetings with the individuals on your list, starting with your #1 pick. If you hear no, (highly, highly unlikely if you are prepared) move on to the next person on your list. Keep asking until you hear yes, then start listening, learning, producing and drafting.

Chapter 3 Be Ridiculously Coachable

The USA Paralympic swim trials for the London 2012 Paralympic Games were held in June. Hundreds of athletes who had been swimming and training countless hours a day for months and years on end competed to find out whether their dreams and hard work would culminate in a trip to London to represent the United States of America. My daughter was one of those swimmers.

This was her second trip to the trials. Four years ago she was a white-faced 12-year-old competing on a playing field she'd never experienced before. She'd barely squeaked in a qualifying time to be at the trials and her coach had her compete so she could see what was possible, and to plant the seeds that she too might have what it takes to make the team one day. It was the first time the Paralympic coaches had a chance to see her in the water and assess her as an athlete. One of the coaches sought me out in the stands after the second day. She was frank in her assessment, "She's got huge potential, but she's not coachable. We're giving her stroke technique suggestions and she's not listening. If that doesn't change, she'll have a tough time excelling in the sport."

On the way home from those trials, I had a long

conversation with Reilly about feedback, coaching and success. I shared the feedback I'd gotten about her from the Paralympic coach. She absorbed, she thought, she changed. Fast forward to today. She's one of the most coachable athletes on her teams and because of that, she increased her performance to the level that she was named alternate to the 2012 Paralympic Team at 16 years old. She learned as a teenager one of the most powerful secrets of the successful; be ridiculously coachable.

If you're not seeking feedback and taking action on what you learn, you'll stay stuck in your behavior ruts, bound to repeat the same scenarios again and again in an endless circle heading nowhere. Let's leave that to the ponies at the petting zoo, shall we? Instead, stay in a highly coachable frame of mind. I once had two CEO clients talking about feedback they'd received from their teams on their leadership. One was lamenting the fact that she didn't have 'perfect' scores to which the other responded, "I *hate it* when they don't give me anything to work on. I can't get better that way." Brilliant! That's as coachable as you can get, and she had the successful career and life to show for it.

What is it about being coachable and seeking feedback that's so important to success? Feedback helps you see past the rough sketch of where you are and opens up what you can become. It helps you stretch your thinking and paint a picture of what is possible if you are willing to put in the work. Honest feedback is one of the greatest gifts you can receive. Without feedback, your full potential might never be realized. A part of growth is being open to this combination. You need to see feedback as a vehicle for showing you how much you are capable of, while at the same time taking in and acting on the feedback you need to get out of your own way and succeed.

There's a lot of head trash that can get in the way of being coachable. Most of us were brought up with the idea that things fit into the boxes of right/wrong and good/bad. Being right equaled being a good kid. Being wrong equaled being bad kid. We can still see and feel the big, red corrections on our schoolwork, or our parent's voices telling us they are disappointed in our behavior. When it's written in black and white like this you can see how screwed up that thinking is. Most people still run with that flawed paradigm though. If being coachable means seeking out feedback on things we're doing "wrong," it's completely contrary to our wiring. Most people have spent years *avoiding* feedback for this very reason!

Women at the top know the real deal though. The more coachable they are, the more feedback they seek, the more they stretch and improve, the more success they can attain. At Moxie, we have a saying that if we don't know it's broken or not working, we can't fix it. That goes for everything from our marketing to my leadership. I formally ask my team at our quarterly strategy sessions what I should keep doing, start doing and stop doing and informally ask them throughout the year. I encourage my team to share the love and let me know when I'm screwing up. And they do. And sometimes it stings. And I always learn something from their feedback. Their ideas are invaluable and I strive to get out of my own way so we can succeed as an organization and I can grow as a leader.

Successful women also understand that being coachable means playing to your strengths. It means being in endless pursuit of getting better at what you're already good at. If you focus only on the areas where you need to improve, you'll get only slightly better. I'll use myself as an example. It's likely that I'm never going to be great at managing details, though it's something I continue to work on improving. Even if I become better than average in this area, it won't really change things significantly for me. However, I am already great at taking big ideas and turning them into actionable processes and tools, and I'm endlessly seeking out ideas and feedback on how I can become a true master in this area. If I continue to work on improving this skill, it's game changing.

Being coachable then, means continually *seeking out*

feedback. High performers create a steady stream of input from the people around them. It's laughable to them to think about only getting feedback on an annual basis. They go well beyond 'formal' systems and create their own eco-system for getting ideas and examples on how they can improve. They create atmospheres of trust around them and frame up feedback as a wonderful, powerful leadership and growth tool, not something punitive and threatening. They listen, they thank the people giving them the feedback, they plan and they act. Then they start the cycle again. They seek out feedback in an on-going spiral of upward performance. They are ridiculously coachable.

Chapter 3 Power Moves

1. Before you do anything else, make sure you fundamentally believe that feedback is a gift and is the fuel of high performers.

2. Take a long look in the mirror. Assess how you've behaved when given feedback in the past. Rate yourself on a scale of 1-5 on how coachable you are. What would it take to make your number a 5?

3. Go through experiences where you have stumbled and identify patterns of behavior that led to those challenges. Be honest with yourself. Debrief your ideas with people

who were involved or knew about the situations to see if you are targeting true areas for improvement that will make a difference for your long-term success and leadership.

4. Re-read your list of strengths, talents and accomplishments. Pick 1-2 behaviors or skills that if you improved upon would catapult you forward. Then create an action plan for improvement.

5. Start seeking feedback on a regular basis. Pull out your calendar, right now, and schedule at least one time block per quarter for getting feedback from your team.

Chapter 4 Surround Yourself With Brilliance

About two years ago, I was honored to spend an evening celebrating the launch of a good friend's business. She'd spent about a year getting things off the ground and had recently gone live with her offering. This was not her first time at the rodeo; she was already a successful, highly regarded leader. She'd invited her tribe to the celebration and there were some great stories that night about how the gathered entourage had collectively helped get this new business rolling. It had come in the form of advice, connections, support, expertise and positive pressure to keep moving forward, to name a few. These were people she trusted, spent time with, learned from and felt supported by.

When I looked around the room, I could tell that she was in on the secret that if you surround yourself with brilliant people who are always looking to get better, your expectations of yourself get bigger, and your own performance improves. You're not going to get that if you're hanging at the water cooler, Facebook page, or news source that's loaded with toxic business associates. Part of thriving, leading and succeeding is being very, very picky about who you are allowing to influence your business, leadership and life thinking. The same goes for who is playing in your sandbox with you. They had better be extraordinary people.

To a person every single successful woman I've interviewed talked about how important having a strong team around her, professionally and personally, has been to her success.

Building a brilliant team does not happen by magic. You need to be very intentional about seeking out and building meaningful relationships with other people out to do big things. As the saying goes, "If you are the smartest person in the room, you're in the wrong room." It could also mean you have not been paying attention to creating and nurturing strong, positive relationships with kick butt people. That really is the case for most people. They simply have not thought about who is on their success team. They underestimate the influence of the people around them, and drift in with the crowd from work, their neighborhood, and their families.

Here's the real deal. The people in your life are either holding you back, or lifting you up. There really is no neutral in this case. It's time to assess your team and commit to surrounding yourself with excellence. Have you ever watched a group of squirrels chasing around in the treetops? They seem to be egging one another on, in a great big game of 'go for it.' The chatter of the other squirrels usually accompanies their jumps from skinny branch to skinny branch. That's what surrounding yourself with brilliance does for you. Most people are clinging to the trunk of the tree, in the 'safe but boring, every day looks pretty much the same' place because they are surrounding themselves with mediocrity. They're not around people going for the treetops. When I watch my own brilliant team going for it, learning new things, taking big leaps as leaders and professionals, it gives me the courage and juice to do the same.

You picked up this book, so you're already successful. Chances are, you have a good number of people around you who are on the success and leadership path with you. In those cases, you need to be purposeful about keeping that core group of people on your team and really nurture those relationships. Many of the women I interviewed talked about having long-term friends and associates who always pushed them to get better. They don't take those relationships for granted, and attribute many of their gains to that support.

It's likely that you also need to add some new players into the mix. The harsh reality is that as we grow and learn, we tend to outgrow some of the people around us. They've hit a level they are comfortable with and put on the cruise control, while you still have the gas pedal all the way to the floor. If you keep circling back to where they are, to their level of success, you'll be holding yourself back. This is one of the toughest lessons I had to learn about success and it took me a long time to get it. You can't keep moving forward if the majority of people around you are not in momentum, too. I am not suggesting you kick those people to the curb. I am suggesting that you understand their influence on your growth and limit that influence.

It's actually easier than it seems to find brilliant people to surround yourself with because you'll find that most people are not interested in going this deep. Remember, they're in 'drift mode.' They want to shove a card in your hands, give you their elevator speech and stumble on to the next person they see. However there are always people like you who are learners, doers and leaders.

One of the secrets of high performing women that separate them from the rest is that they view forming and nurturing real connections with smart, successful people as a key skill they continue to hone. They spend time thinking about who is on their team and how they can serve those people to help them grow. They are genuine in their love and respect for the people on their team. Yes, love. They operate by the principle that if you wouldn't fight to keep someone on your team, they shouldn't be on your team.

They also always, always have their radar up for people to add to their team. They view the process of making new, meaningful connections a little like you might view serious dating. They know they want to be in a long-term relationship with high performers, and they are constantly scanning the environment for likely candidates. Once they've found someone who seems to be playing at their level or above, they take the time to really, *really* find out what the other person is all about. They find out what their wants and needs are, what their unique talents and abilities are and how they fit into the bigger picture. Then they begin to help move the person forward by connecting them to resources, people, ideas and opportunities that matter to them. If they bring them on to their work team, they also do an extraordinary job of getting the hell out of their way so they can go about the business of being brilliant.

Let me share another example. We're renting a house in Spain that's owned by a former Commander of the Royal British Guard. He apparently really, really loved his job and has what I would classify as an obsession with Queen Elizabeth II. Why do I say this? The THIRTEEN large, framed photos of her adorning the walls in the living and dining rooms were a bit of a giveaway. Seriously. Thirteen photos of the Queen Mum.

My first thought after seeing the place was 'Why in the hell would someone want to make their vacation home on the Mediterranean coast in Spain feel like they're in England?'

(Really- think about it.) That was quickly followed by 'This guy needs to get a hobby.' Then it hit me. The photos were born of a deep loyalty and respect for his leader. Even in retirement, she plays a huge part in his life and his affection and esteem remain true even as his years of service have come to a close. It's led to an odd choice in decor, to be sure, but the message is clear; she's a leader he'd do just about anything for.

You only get that when you've done your best in service of your team and, done what I believe is the true mark of a leader, led with authentic respect and love. Queen Elizabeth once said, "I cannot lead you into battle. I do not give you laws or administer justice but I can do something else – I can give my heart and my devotion to these old islands and to all the peoples of our brotherhood of nations." Right on, Lizzie.

*High performance women are able to surround themselves with brilliance because of what they **give** to the individuals on their teams.*

Chapter 4 Power Moves

1. Make a list of the people you spend the most time with. Leave no stone unturned. Think about people from work, home, family, friends, neighborhood, church, sports teams etc. Once you have your list, go through each individual

and honestly assess his or her impact on you. Put a small plus or minus next to their name. Once you have your list, create a plan to nurture relationships with the plus group and limit time or influence from the minus group.

2. Pick 4-5 people from your inner circle and schedule a group lunch. Propose getting together regularly to share ideas and hold one another accountable for growth.

3. Assess the individuals that you work most closely with who report to you, your professional team. Ask yourself, 'Would I fight to keep each one of them?' If the answer is yes, sit down with them as soon as possible and share your appreciation for having them on your team. If you have not already done so, create a plan to nurture their growth. If the answer is no, you need to figure out a plan to get your answer to 'yes' or take action immediately. You're not doing them, or yourself, any favors by keeping them on the team.

4. Create a 'virtual bench', a small group of people that you would love to have on your team if the opportunity arose. Let them know that if they are ever looking to make a move or if you are ever in the position to bring them on board, you would love to have the conversation. In the

meantime, nurture the relationship by scheduling reminders on your calendar to reach out to them in a variety of ways such as phone calls, emails and in-person meetings.

5. Pay attention and keep your radar up. When you hear someone asking interesting questions, doing interesting things, pushing the envelope, being brilliant in what they do or generally kicking butt, find a way to meet with them as quickly as possible.

Chapter 5 Be a Sponge

Secret number five is what makes successful women leading the way so much damned fun to be around. The secret is that they never, ever think they've 'made it' and have learned enough. They are *always* in learning and growth mode. They are wired for curiosity and have an open mind about possibilities, ideas and options. This goes for their careers and businesses as well as for their own capabilities and knowledge.

The super-super secret is that you don't rise to the top; you learn and grow your way to the top.

It seems obvious, doesn't it? If you're walking around in the world like a sponge for new ideas, you're very likely to hit on some good ones on an on-going basis. And if you're thinking about yourself as a walking, breathing do-it-to-yourself project, you're going to keep asking yourself how you can get better and what you need to learn.

The fact of the matter is that most people are just turning the crank on their career and life. They show up, do about the same thing every day, go home, and do about the same thing every night. They are not in learning and growth mode, they are in stasis. They tune in to television programs, computer games and social media sites in order to tune out for an average of about FOUR hours a night. That is a horrifying waste of time and intellect.

Somehow the majority of people have gotten it in their heads that they can stop 'learning' as soon as they leave the formal school setting. They've been *forced* to attend school, and now their work is done. Women leading the way know just the opposite is true. A whole new opportunity for learning begins the day your formal education ends. You get to choose growth, choose ideas to pursue, choose topics that interest you and move you forward. You can start learning about how you are wired, what your strengths and weaknesses are and your abilities as a leader. I get stoked just writing about it. Our opportunities for learning and growth are literally endless.

Start thinking about the world as a living classroom designed specifically for your learning and growth. Literally everything holds the opportunity for lessons, ideas and forward progress. If you have not done so already, I highly recommend you set a growth plan for yourself to focus your efforts. Think about what skills and experiences you want to add to your repertoire and seek out opportunities and situations that support you getting what you want!

Chapter 5 Power Moves

1. Always be asking yourself growth questions. For example, at the end of every project, big interaction (good and bad), sales call, presentation etc. ask yourself, 'What did I learn from that?' At the end of each day, ask yourself 'What did I learn today?' Be sure you answer yourself!

2. Turn off your television during the week and limit your time on social media sites like Facebook and Pinterest to 15 minutes a day. I'm not kidding. Spend the time that you would normally piss away, reading a book, an interesting blog or an informative magazine. Meditate or go for a walk. Pick up an old or new hobby, meet with your inner circle, spend time with your family or write in a journal. If you just can't break the addiction, limit yourself to 20 minutes per night, tops.

3. Create an annual growth plan for yourself. Include business topics, hobbies, life skills, you name it. Update it quarterly and review your progress.

4. Start or join a business book club. Anyone who is involved or willing to jump into a group like this is clearly on a learning and growth path like you, and you'll get the double hit of learning *and* surrounding yourself with

brilliance.

5. Engage in an activity I call a Full On 45. Focus on learning about a topic or improving a skill/ability in one area for 45 days. Every single day of the 45 days you must do at least one thing every day to learn or improve in that area. No weekend or holiday breaks allowed. Keep a chart so you can track your progress. You'll be amazed.

Conclusion: Pulling It All Together

It's up to you now, sister. Remember that success and leadership are about thinking the right way and doing the right things, consistently. I've shared the Five Secrets, and outlined 25 Power Moves for you. Don't be a victim of the knowing-doing gap I talked about earlier. Take ACTION. Work your way through the Rock Your Moxie: Power Moves for Women Leading the Way series and check in with me along the way. I want to know how you're doing as you move forward, and hear your stories of success. Send me an email or join in the conversation on my blog:

Mo@moxieexchange.com

www.moxieexchange.com/blog

I'd also love for you to be a part of the Rock Your Moxie: A Monthly Shot of Leadership & Success community. I lead a monthly online workshop covering the ideas and Power Moves from the books. There's no cost to attend the workshop (remember that part about needing YOU at the table?) and it will really make the content come to life for you. Plus, you're bound to connect with some very interesting and successful women who are getting after it like you.

Now get out there and rock your moxie. I've got your back!

The 25 Power Moves

Own It, Create It

1. Create a list of your strengths, abilities and successes. Keep it in a handy place in an easily updateable format. Review it and add to it quarterly.

2. Ask five people to share what they believe your professional and leadership strengths are. Do not ask your parents! You won't believe them, because you'll think they're inherently biased, which they should be. If they are not, you shouldn't want to know what they think anyway! The five should include a mix of people in your world, such as a boss/former boss, co-worker, employee or direct report, good friend and your partner. Write down their responses and add them to your own list.

3. Get a group of 5-6 kick butt professional women together. Let them know in advance that each of you will be sharing things you are good at, strengths you have and recent accomplishments. Provide wine if it's slow going at first! Joking aside, make sure each of you can articulate in a strong way what you're good at. This practice will help you 'own it' in real-world scenarios.

4. Create three lists in relation to your work and professional development: things to start doing, stop doing and stay the

course on. Pick one each week to take action on.

5. At the end of each day, review your calendar. What action do you need to take based on what happened in your day? No more than three things should make the cut, so make them worth your time and energy.

Learn to Draft

1. Identify the people in your life who have served as your mentors or sponsors in the past. Reach out to them and thank them, sharing specifics about how their involvement in your professional life helped you succeed. Everybody loves and deserves to know they've had a positive impact!

2. Get over yourself. If you try and do it all solo, you're slowing down your growth and the potential impact you can have on the world. Get comfortable with the idea of having sponsors.

3. Pay attention and recognize the sponsorship relationships that are happening all around you. Who is involved? How do the mechanics seem to work in your company, community and/or industry? Get familiar with the 'cultural norms' of sponsorship relationships in your particular corner of the world so you know how to play well in that sandbox.

4. Identify 3-4 people in your organization, community or industry who are 2-3 steps ahead of where you are. They

should be sitting in a place where you want to go and be someone you admire.

5. Ask. Sets up meetings with the individuals on your list, starting with your #1 pick. If you hear no, (highly, highly unlikely if you are prepared) move on to the next person on your list. Keep asking until you hear yes, then start listening, learning, producing and drafting.

Be Ridiculously Coachable

1. Before you do anything else, make sure you fundamentally believe that feedback is a gift and is the fuel of high performers.

2. Take a long look in the mirror. Assess how you've behaved when given feedback in the past. Rate yourself on a scale of 1-5 on how coachable you are. What would it take to make your number a 5?

3. Go through experiences where you have stumbled and identify patterns of behavior that led to those challenges. Be honest with yourself. Debrief your ideas with people who were involved or knew about the situations to see if you are targeting true areas for improvement that will make a difference for your long-term success and leadership.

4. Re-read your list of strengths, talents and accomplishments. Pick 1-2 behaviors or skills that if you

improved upon would catapult you forward. Then create an action plan for improvement.

5. Start seeking feedback on a regular basis. Pull out your calendar, right now, and schedule at least one time block per quarter for getting feedback from your team.

Surround Yourself With Brilliance

1. Make a list of the people you spend the most time with. Leave no stone unturned. Think about people from work, home, family, friends, neighborhood, church, sports teams etc. Once you have your list, go through each individual and honestly assess his or her impact on you. Put a small plus or minus next to their name. Once you have your list, create a plan to nurture relationships with the plus group and limit time or influence from the minus group.

2. Pick 4-5 people from your inner circle and schedule a group lunch. Propose getting together regularly to share ideas and hold one another accountable for growth.

3. Assess the individuals that you work most closely with who report to you, your professional team. Ask yourself, 'Would I fight to keep each one of them?' If the answer is yes, sit down with them as soon as possible and share your appreciation for having them on your team. If you have not already done so, create a plan to nurture their growth. If the answer is no, you need to figure out a plan to get your

answer to 'yes' or take action immediately. You're not doing them, or yourself, any favors by keeping them on the team.

4. Create a 'virtual bench', a small group of people that you would love to have on your team if the opportunity arose. Let them know that if they are ever looking to make a move or if you are ever in the position to bring them on board, you would love to have the conversation. In the meantime, nurture the relationship by scheduling reminders on your calendar to reach out to them in a variety of ways such as phone calls, emails and in-person meetings.

5. Pay attention and keep your radar up. When you hear someone asking interesting questions, doing interesting things, pushing the envelope, being brilliant in what they do or generally kicking butt, find a way to meet with them as quickly as possible.

Be a Sponge

1. At the end of every day, ask yourself this question, 'What did I learn today?' Be sure you answer yourself!

2. Turn off your television during the week and limit your time on social media sites like Facebook and Pinterest to 15 minutes a day. I'm not kidding. Spend the time that you would normally piss away reading a book, an interesting

blog or an informative magazine. Meditate or go for a walk. Pick up an old or new hobby, meet with your inner circle, spend time with your family or write in a journal. If you just can't break the addiction, limit yourself to 20 minutes per night, tops.

3. Create an annual growth plan for yourself. Include business topics, hobbies, life skills, you name it. Update it quarterly and review your progress.

4. Start or join a business book club. Anyone who is involved or willing to jump into a group like this is clearly on a learning and growth path like you, and you'll get the double hit of learning *and* surrounding yourself with brilliance.

5. Engage in an activity I call a Full On 45. Focus on learning about a topic or improving a skill/ability in one area for 45 days. Every single day of the 45 days you must do at least one thing every day to learn or improve in that area. No weekend or holiday breaks allowed. Keep a chart so you can track your progress. You'll be amazed.

No 2

Rock your *Moxie*

Power Moves for Women Leading the Way

5 **Strategies** *for* Warp Speed Growth

by Maureen Berkner Boyt

Rock Your Moxie:

Power Moves for Women Leading the Way

5 Strategies for Warp Speed Growth

Maureen Berkner Boyt

Table of Contents

Click here to join a community of women in an online monthly workshop covering ideas and Power Moves from the book

Chapter 1 Live On the Skinny Branches

————————◆————————

When is the last time that you've done something that really made you feel alive? That you thought to yourself, 'I can't believe I'm actually doing this!' while in the moment. Something that took your breath away in its audacity. When? Have you been heeding Eleanor Roosevelt's advice to "Do one thing every day that scares you."?

As far as I know, complete strangers in Japan, Germany and the US have naked photos of me. A few weeks back, in the pouring rain, I stripped down and jumped off a small cliff into the Fairy Pools on the Isle of Skye with the small knot of bystanders, who materialized when I started shedding clothes, snapping photos. I knew the water would be so cold it would literally take my breath away (at 6C/43F it did), that I would need to get naked in front of strangers (I did) and that I would have to face one of my big fears (heights) to take the plunge.

Not only did I jump, I got out, scrambled back up the rocks and cliff and jumped AGAIN for good measure. Hell yeah, sister. I was ALIVE! I leapt for the sheer wild joy of it. I jumped so my kids could see me face a fear and do it anyway. I jumped to prove to myself that I could, and that, as I said to my husband with a wink when we walked off down the path after my jumps, "I've still got it." Twenty years ago I took a similar plunge into the Colorado River and I needed to prove to myself that although I am more responsible these days, I am just as fearless.

I took the plunge because I knew if I didn't I would always think to myself, "I should have." Those folks with the photos of me have photos. I have the experience and visceral reminder that the good stuff in life, those big experiences, aren't going to happen unless you're willing to take the plunge. One of the Germans with a camera, a guy of about 25 said, "You are crazy, girl!", as I was heading back for round 2. You're damned straight I am, Skippy! I am crazy - full of life, ideas, action and forward momentum. I am willing to do something that scares me to get the big rewards. That's the key.

If you want to grow fast, it's not going to happen if you're playing it safe.

A key strategy for kicking it into high gear is getting out there on what I call *the skinny branches*. You know the place I'm talking about. The high risk, high reward, I've-never-been-here-before domain. For those willing to go there, it's really an extraordinary place to learn and grow as a leader and a person. It's a place high performers seek out and spend a LOT of time in.

To get out on skinny branches you have to face failure and fear, so most people stay in the safe, slow-growth zone. That 1-2 punch is too much for them to stomach. An even bigger nut to crack can be getting over your fear OF failure. Leaders, though, have totally different paradigms for fear and failure. They understand that high performance involves being comfortable with taking risk and failing *into* success. They get it that failure is a part of the growth and success equation. Nobody gets it right every, single time unless they are doing exactly the same things in exactly the same ways that they always have. That's a pattern of stagnation. It's very predictable, and will get you exactly nowhere. Think of failure instead as an accelerator, rather than as something you spend energy trying to avoid. It's simply an expected part of the process of growth and if you're not failing, it's an indication that you're not growing.

If you want fast growth, you also have to be willing to move through fear. Amelia Earhart said it beautifully, "Our fears are paper tigers." The majority of our fears are self-imposed. They exist only between our own oars. The fact of the matter is we manufacture every fear we have except that of loud noises and falling, which we are born with. Research has found that we can pretty quickly pick up 'evolutionary fears' of things that really can potentially harm us (snakes, spiders, heights, water) because those fears can serve to protect us. Other than that, it's all you, baby. Here's the beautiful thing about getting those manufactured fears under control; they hate the light of day. Fears have their tightest grip on us when we continue to spin them in our own minds. So don't. Talk about them with someone. Name them. Get clear on what's behind your fear. Once you name a fear and bring it out for review, the power that fear exerts decreases exponentially.

Slightly over 6 months after The Moxie Exchange Movement launched, we held our first mentoring event for teenaged girls, MoxieFest. That put me WAY out on the skinny branches. We took a risk- we didn't have the time or the money to pull it off, and we still went for it because it was in alignment with our values and what's important to us. Holding the event so quickly was a reminder that the timing will NEVER be right, and that we have to do things that make us uncomfortable. I had all sorts of between-the-ears fears about why we shouldn't hold MoxieFest, but when I really dug in and looked at them, I understood that they were all self-imposed. They were 'trunk clinging' thoughts and a great example of the limits we tend to set for ourselves that serve to slow our growth. Sure, there were little screw-ups during that first event but we used those small failures from year one to make year two of the event even more powerful.

Here's one more strategy for living on the skinny branches, failing forward and slaying your fears: don't forget to laugh. I've made some epic dives from the skinny branches. I'm talking crash and burn stupid moves. I've taken a page from my teenaged son Caiden's book on this one. He likes to MUni (mountain-unicycle). Yup, you read that right; he rides steep, gnarly mountain trails on one wheel. When he goes down, he goes down *hard*. When he comes up, he's bleeding AND laughing at the same time, usually with a "Did you SEE that?" whoop of joy. If you're going to dig it, enjoy the crash, because if you spend too much time licking your wounds or beating yourself up, you won't get out there again anytime soon. When Cade goes down, he doesn't give up, head home, and shove his MUni in the garage because he fell. He doesn't sit in the trail and berate himself for wiping out. He doesn't take the easier choice in routes after he bites it. He makes sure someone *saw* his crash, he laughs, he figures out why he crashed and then he hops back on and heads back up the trail.

The hell with fear, then! To hell with seeing failure as terminal! Kick those thoughts to the curb and press on. Get out there on the skinny branches. Do something TODAY to feel alive and strong conquer your fears. Climb out there on the skinny branches and stretch yourself and watch your growth start to soar!

Chapter 1 Power Moves

1. Pick a decision you've found yourself holding back on and playing it safe about, and create a 'worst case scenario' chart to help you move forward. At the top, write down the decision, with three columns below it. In column 1, write down the worst case scenario, in column 2, how you'll know you've gotten there/indicators you have reached the worst case, in column 3 what action you will take.

2. Host a lunch/happy hour in honor of your biggest screw up. Own, celebrate, laugh, and discuss when things didn't go as planned. Share what you learned and how the 'failure' has helped move you forward.

3. Name your fears and talk them down. "If I do "x" I'm afraid that "y" will happen."

4. Do a debrief on the things you're initially categorizing as a 'failure'. Answer these questions: What went right? What did I learn? How did I just fail forward toward success?

5. Have a fan club. Yes, a fan club. Have a few key people from your inner circle that you have set up an explicit arrangement with in advance so they understand their role. When you are feeling fearful or worried about failing, call them up or meet with them to say, "This is scaring the

crap out of me!" or, "I'm about to go really, really big on this one." Their job is to tell you that you are a brilliant rock star, you've got this, and that they are holding the safety net for you. They are not there to go through contingency plans, or cost benefit analysis. They are there to push your butt out on the skinny branch and cheer you on. Trust me, it works.

Chapter 2 Suck It Up and Shake It Off

———————————————

What awaits you when you walk into a Paralympic swim meet? Prosthetic legs strewn about the pool deck. Guide dogs. Empty wheelchairs. And elite athletes in action making it all look easy. The sheer athleticism of the group is an incredible sight to see. What you won't find, and what I've never heard, are excuses or whining. No complaining that things are too hard, that something hurts, that they should be given a break. Trust me; this group would have every right to do that and more. Many of them live with daily pain. All of them live with some form of physical disability ranging from almost full paralysis, to missing limbs to blindness. Yet there's not a whiner to be found in the group.

Life can be hard. Leadership *is* hard. Sometimes we have to do things we simply don't like or be in situations we would rather take a pass on. Life can serve up some truly crappy circumstances. How should we handle it? As my good friend Sara once told me, *"Suck it up, cupcake!"*

I've been known to whine occasionally in my life. Actually, my brother and sisters used to call me "Screamin' " when I was little because I would scream until I fainted when I was angry or things weren't going my way. (Cut me a little slack- I stopped that charming practice when I was 3, but the nicknamed endured.) As for early in my career, what did complaining get me? It certainly didn't win me any points with co-workers, and it didn't improve my mindset any. My internal dialogue of 'that's not fair' or 'this is hard' only served as a governor on my ability to lead and succeed. It was, and remains, a losing practice.

If you want to grow fast, leave the bitching, complaining, excuses and whining in the dust.

When I feel the urge to complain, I ask myself a series of questions to get my attitude and mindset pointed forward and up. 'This is hard compared to *what*?' 'Is anyone going to die?' 'Am I going to learn something from the challenge?' Every time I end up with the same conclusion- time to suck it up, learn a lesson, if there is one and move on. Nobody wants to hear your drama or woes. Really. They don't. If you feel obliged to share, you're shooting yourself in the success, career and business foot. Knock it off. Think about the most successful women you know. How much time to they spend complaining about their challenges or circumstances? I'll throw down for another bottle of Spanish wine and wager that your answer will be very, very little to none. They are focused forward, not spending energy on complaining and excuses.

My daughter had a swim race recently that can only be

described as ugly. Her technique was terrible and her time was slower than anything she'd raced in years. It was a bit painful to watch. It was also very public, with her name and race time up on the scoreboard for all to see. Oh, and she was almost naked at the time as race suits these days seem to consist of about 4 square inches of fabric. So, we had a 15- year old, mostly naked girl failing in public, which would seem to add up to a recipe for a very big meltdown. Not so. I knew she was going to be just fine because she has an incredible ability to shake things off. It's almost astonishing how fully she leaves it all in the pool, bad or good.

I love watching her at the end of a race. She touches the wall and immediately looks up at the clock. Either a wide grin spreads across her face or she gives a small headshake, depending on what the numbers read. Then she hops out of the pool, shakes herself off, and heads over to cool down and talk with her coaches. When the race is done, it's done. She takes it in, debriefs on what worked and what didn't, and moves on. She doesn't beat herself up or replay the tape again and again in her head when a race goes bad. When it goes well, she enjoys the moment. She's got the mental toughness that it takes to succeed in sports.

At 16, she's mastered what it has taken me years to learn. Failures, a mistake, a bad call in business or leadership are all things to learn from, shake off and move beyond. Sara Blakely of

Spanx attributes failure as one of her top success tools. In the last chapter I talked about failing forward. Here's the other half the equation; it's not just our ability to fail but also *our ability to fail PLUS the ability to quickly shake it off and move on that accelerates our success.*

I spent years failing, and then beating the hell out of myself mentally for the failures. Yes, I had learned from the failures and was farther along, but somehow I had missed the part about letting it go, too. I could have won a gold medal in mental self-flagellation. I wasted a lot of mental energy replaying tapes in my head of my failures and mistakes.

Watching my daughter shake it off after a bad race has been an eye-opener for me. She fails, she learns, she moves on. All the learning, none of the guilt. It's a beautiful thing. When I start down the mental-replay-punching-bag path, I pull up an image of my daughter at the end of a bad race looking up, hopping out of the pool, and shaking it off. Then I shake it off and move forward, too.

Beware of rolling around in your successes for too long, too. It's an equally dangerous practice. We all know people who bring up awards they've won or triumphs they've had in the past. Heck yeah I want to celebrate my wins and the wins of others, but not past their expiration date. Watching my daughter shake it off after a great race has been as eye opening as watching her after a bad race. Fist pump, smile, cool down, debrief, time to move on and get focused on the next race. If you're focused on the past, whether good or bad, you're taking your eye off forward momentum and progress.

Chapter 2 Power Moves

1. Take all your gripes, complaints, slights, bad blood, excuses, health issues etc and write them on individual slips of paper. Really purge. Get it all out. Place them in a fireplace or fireproof container (old coffee cans work great), light a match, drop it in, burn the hell out of them and ceremonially LET THEM GO. I've done this with everyone from highly successful executives to teenagers and every time it's pure magic.

2. Tune in to the conversations you are a part of. You're going to be amazed how much victim talk surrounds you. Make a vow to not chime in when excuses, blame, or complaints come up. Either change the conversation or walk away.

3. When you feel the urge to throw a pity party bubbling up, ask yourself these three questions: "This is hard compared to *what*? Is anyone going to die? What am I supposed to

learn from this?"

4. When you find yourself replaying a failure, literally tell yourself, "Stop! We've moved on from that." Refocus by rewriting a goal you are working on. Determine two clear action items, that you can complete by the end of the day, toward accomplishing that goal.

5. Create visual prompts or mental cues to remind yourself to suck it up and shake it off. Photos, screen savers, and vivid memories that you can draw up quickly all work well.

Chapter 3 Pay To Play

Women spend a *lot* of money on clothes, hair and coffee. The averages, for example, $50,000 on hair in a lifetime, are really staggering. We'll write big fat checks at the drop of the hat for our kids to play competitive sports, get music lessons, or have the latest gaming technology. We'll help a friend, or a complete stranger through charitable giving. But ask women to invest in our own learning and growth and suddenly things are WAY too expensive.

There are a multitude of reasons for this, depending on the woman. They range from fear of actually having to show up and make real change, fear of showing up and feeling inadequate, not understanding that if you don't learn and grow your career or business won't either, setting a 'deserving' level that is set really low, feeling guilty that investing time and money in her own growth is somehow selfish and so forth.

There is a real difference here between men and women. For men it's not whether they're going to invest in themselves, it's about "Where?" and "How much?" They're ready, willing, and able to spend money and time to move the dial for themselves, in many different ways. Case in point: men will drop thousands of dollars and hundreds of hours a year on golf. Golf. Why? Because they know that not only is it a good time, it's a good investment in their careers. They can connect the dots between the putting green and building relationships, getting the latest information on what's happening in the business community and sealing some deals. They unapologetically put themselves in as many learning and growth environments as they can, knowing that doing so equals increased exposure to people, ideas, tools and success. They will drop the money and invest the time for a seminar or a coach without batting an eye because they know it will help move them forward.

I've been polling organizational development leaders and executive coaches lately about this phenomenon, and to a person they see the same disparity. It's really, really troubling. If we want to see changes in the numbers at the top and in pay equity, we've GOT to be willing to invest time and money in building our own capabilities.

In more blunt terms, you've got to pay to play.

The super successful women in my life have this rapid-growth strategy down. One of the fundamental bedrocks of on-going success is actually having a strategy and plan in place for growth. One of my favorite women in the world started with very little in life and now owns two successful businesses and is an adjunct professor. She shared with me that she spends at least two days a quarter at a seminar or conference, and works on-going with an executive coach. She exemplifies fast-growth women. They budget the dollars, spend the time, and invest in learning. Why? Because they understand that if they want to make more money and be more successful, THEY need to grow. It doesn't happen in reverse order. You've got to grow your way into your success and the fastest way to do that is to make the commitment and investment. One of the greatest gifts we can give the people we love is our own development. As we become more, we can achieve more. We'll have bigger experience and ideas to share with them, and more financial resources to provide for them. The truly selfish act then is to choose NOT to invest in your own growth.

Because you're reading this book, I know you're at least part of the way there. You're interested in growing. You're on the success path. You want more. You're willing to invest in yourself, your relationships, and your development to some degree. My question to you is: are you all in? Are you nickel and diming yourself, or making a real investment? You've got to pay to play. I want you thinking like a guy right now. I want you knowing, feeling, and believing that an investment in your own growth is going ratchet up your success level in a big, big way. Game on.

Chapter 3 Power Moves

1. Add a 'learning and growth' line to your budget. You should be spending at least as much annually on your professional and leadership learning and development as you are on your 'external' brand (clothes, shoes, hair, makeup, jewelry.) The money IS there. It's about making the choice on where you're going to spend it.

2. Subscribe to a few good magazines or blogs that are focused on leadership and success. You'll learn from their content and also find out about good programs and resources by what they are covering.

3. Poll successful women in your life about places they go for learning and growth. Ask them what organizations, programs and resources have contributed to their growth and success.

4. Commit 30 minutes a day to learning. Block it in your calendar.

5. Start a learning library. Start building up books, audios etc. that have been recommended to you as growth building blocks.

Chapter 4 Get Your Happy On

Whenever I start to take myself too seriously, I wear pigtails. It's really hard to get stressed out or be a downer when you're sporting the hairstyle you wore when you were three. Trust me on this. I also reach out to women who fill me up and make me laugh. It always works. By making the choice to create an environment where I feel happy (pigtails) and surrounding myself with happy people (funny, smart girlfriends), my mood gets much lighter and I'm back on track.

We now know that when you're laughing, you're learning. We also know that who you hang around really impacts how you feel. Some smarty-pants researchers at Harvard and UC San Diego proved it, in case you were thinking this whole happiness thing is a load of crap. Go ahead and do your own little experiment if you like. Seek out and spend an hour with the happiest people you know and pay attention to how much better you feel after that hour. Their affect on you is a little like being sprinkled with happy dust.

A buckle-your-seatbelt growth strategy is to BE the happy person people seek out. You see, as Colin Powel said, "Perpetual optimism is a force multiplier." When you get your happy on, in a genuine way, possibilities seem endless. Your energy is up and the people around you get in the believing state of mind, too. Your joy creates an ecosystem around you of forward momentum, laughter and creativity.

Two of the most optimistic, genuine, friendly women I know are Kelli Tangney Williams and Katy Piotrowski. I can recall for you *exactly* when I met both of these women, even though it's been almost 25 years since I met Kelli and 10 years since I met Katy. They both light up a room, and you want to be around them. You want to hear what they have to say. You want to drink whatever is in their Kool-Aid and see if you can get seconds, too. THAT is as powerful as it gets. Not surprisingly they are both very successful in their chosen paths, have strong relationships with their families and are respected and loved by the people in their lives. *Happiness is a strategy for success!*

Kelli and I were college roommates and occasionally she'd get what she called 'the Sunday night blues.' On those Sunday evenings she'd start to get quiet, and a little morose, that the weekend was over and it was back to class, homework and work in a few hours. It was like someone threw a dimmer switch on over our entire apartment. All of us were a little quieter. All of us got glum. Holy influence, Batgirl! I learned from her that when you consistently bring your joy you elevate the people around you into feeling that way, too. Equally important was that if you're the person people are expecting happiness from, it can throw them off if you hit a glum patch. Luckily, I also learned that peanut butter and chocolate milk would perk Kelli right back up and get her back on track. She didn't need much, nor do any of us if we want to turn it around, to get back to optimistic and happy.

Think of ways you can amp up the joy in your business or department, too, because it turns out happy workplaces beat the pants off unhappy companies in profitability, retention, lost time and a host of other factors. Kris Boesch, Founder of Choose People, has the best blog out there on having happy employees. Her company completed 1,000 hours of research and they have the secret sauce (8 key factors) for creating an organization where people feel good about coming to work. I'll take fries with that secret sauce, please!

We've had a lot of people comment on the energy and happiness that surrounds The Moxie Exchange Movement. What a compliment! We really have set out to build an organization where you don't have to check your fun-factor at the door. We know we can drive business results faster and farther when we're in an atmosphere of joy. You can really be a 'serious' business organization or 'serious' about your career and leadership and still have fun. Life's too short to go to another boring business meeting, or be a part of a boring organization. Been there, done that, got the tee shirt. The person who best articulated what we're doing was Simone Marean, the Executive Director of the Girl's Leadership Institute. She looked at me and simply said, "There's strength in joy." Yes, yes, yes! That is it *exactly*. Choosing joy is choosing strength and choosing growth.

Seriously, this should not come as a shock. Think about when your best ideas came to you or the teams you were working with were really cranking it out. What bosses have you really given it your all for? What companies have you worked for that you really loved? When have you seen the people in your life really responding to you and helping you succeed, how were you showing up? The thread of optimism and happiness will be woven throughout those scenarios.

As always, it circles back to choice. How you're showing up, whom you're hanging out with, what you're doing as a company. Think about what you're doing in business and in life to create joy and growth for yourself and those around you. Remember that there's strength in joy.

I'll give you extra credit if you send me a picture of you in pigtails!

Chapter 4 Power Moves

1. Wake up every day and choose happiness and joy. If you get off track, remember that you can choose again. Create joy in your world.

2. Pick one thing to keep with you that is guaranteed to make you smile. I used to carry a small picture of my husband's high school graduation photo with me (he was wearing a blue velvet tux) and would pull it out when I needed a lift.

3. Get really interested in other people and tuned in to their emotions, especially the people closest to you. Figure out the things that you do consistently and authentically that make you and other people feel good. Do more of them.

4. Choose your news media carefully. Sensationalism and fear sell, so that's what the news is loaded with. Watching it has a big impact on your well- being. Consider skimming only headlines from a few different sources.

5. Build some silliness into your life. For example, on Friday mornings I hold what is known in our household as 'Friday morning dance party.' I turn on bad 80's music and shake my bootie all around the kitchen. My teenagers, who are wiped out by that point of the week truly *cannot* stop themselves from laughing, and I feel great, too.

Chapter 5 Ask Until Your Knees Shake

⸻

Are you willing to leave 2 million dollars on the table? Because women ask for raises and promotions 85% less often than men, and when they do ask, it's for 35% less, so we're doing just that! Because women ask less, and ask *for* less, the financial implications over our careers are staggering. This doesn't just apply to money. We're asking for less and negotiating about less across the board. We don't ask for choice assignments, or lower interest rates, or more dollars to finance our businesses or travel upgrades. And we get what we ask for.

Linda Babcock and Sara Laschever have written two brilliant books on the topic that I highly recommend you read -- *Women Don't Ask* and *Ask For It.*. The first is more about the research and findings on women and negotiations; the second is more of a 'how to.' They found two key factors that contribute to women negotiating less and asking for less: *women don't realize what opportunities for negotiation exist and are worried about the social consequences of asking.*

My first job out of college was with an incredible company working for an extraordinary leader. There was an economic recession at the time, and college graduates were finding it hard to land jobs. I remember it like it was yesterday - my new boss offering me the position and telling me the salary, $18,000 annually. I felt *lucky* to have landed the job and *never even considered asking for more money*, even though I was making significantly more money per hour in my waitressing job. Fast forward a few months to a conversation with one of my male friends and co-workers who started at the same time and in the same role. He was making $24,000 a year. Why? Because he asked. I didn't, he did, and he got $6,000 more a year in his pocket.

Even after I found this out, I didn't ask for a raise because I didn't want to seem greedy, and I knew that the economy was rocky at the time. I was a classic case study for women and negotiations. I didn't know I could or should ask for more money in the first place, and even when I knew I should be making more, I was worried I would seem like a money-grubber. If only I knew then what I know now.

You have got to start asking for things at a level that seems ludicrous to you. You've got to ask until your knees shake. When you start to do this, and understand that asking is a key strategy for growth, prosperity and success, you will see all of those things skyrocket for you.

When you next have the opportunity to ask for a raise or

negotiate a fee, get a number in your head. Now add 35%. You're probably just hitting the range that your male co-worker or competitor is asking for. What's the worst that can happen? If you are prepared, are 'likeable' in your negotiations (sadly the research shows this is key to our success in this regard) and state your case clearly, you are probably going to get very close to what you are asking for. Even if you hear a flat-out no, you are no worse off than you were before you asked! You are in the exact same place you were before you asked!

I painfully watched the male/female difference play out again recently with my own kids, who were about to start working for my husband. He asked them both how much they thought they should make per hour, and had them tell him independently what their salary requests were. My daughter: $8 per hour. My son: $12 per hour. When he asked their reasoning, our daughter shared that she was happy to have the job and that she didn't want to impact the cash flow of the business too much. Our son was all about how having him around would be a huge help to his dad and that he deserved at least that amount... and could he have a cut of profits, too? Classic female/male behavior.

My husband knew about the research, so went back to them for round two. He asked them again how much they thought they should make, asking if their first number was their final number. He even prompted my daughter to focus on the positive impact she would have on the business when coming up with her number. This time around my son asked for $100 an hour. Straight-faced. He had reasons, and a formula for why he really should make that much, and probably wouldn't take the job if he wasn't going to make that hourly rate. My daughter? $12.

I am not a shrinking violet and neither is my daughter. People have used phrases like 'force of nature' to describe both of us, yet we both sold ourselves short in a massive way. I share these personal examples because I believe that negotiations and asking for less is something that it's easy to intellectualize. You might be thinking, "Oh yes. I've heard about this." Here's my slap upside the head wake-up call for you:

You've been burned by this too. These statistics are about YOU.

You have got to own that this impacts you and commit to changing it for yourself. Our society has wired girls and women from a very young age not to ask and not to negotiate. There is good news, though. A good part of this battle is about understanding the issue and then about learning a new skill and implementing behavior changes.

It's also about recognizing our own biases that it's okay for men to ask, and not acceptable for women. Each of us needs to take a long, hard look in the mirror and see how we are contributing to the issue. Are you saying 'yes' to women as frequently as you are to men? Are you encouraging the women in your life to ask for more? Are you paying the women in your organization as much as the men? Giving them the same stretch opportunities? We didn't get to these stats in a vacuum. You need to start asking until your knees shake, and making it okay, even encouraging it for other women, too.

Chapter 5 Power Moves

1. Change your mindset and start to think about just about everything as negotiable. You'll be amazed at what's possible. Babcock suggests starting small, and practicing. Ask the cleaners to have your clothes ready a day earlier, ask if there's a fresher cut of fish at the market, ask for an even lower rate at the hotel and an even later check-out.

2. Become a master negotiator. Set a goal for yourself to become an expert (or at least proficient) on negotiations. Take a class. Read up on negotiation skills and practice, practice, practice.

3. Share the research and results with your daughters

and colleagues. Mentor young women on how to ask and negotiate.

4. Watch how you're responding to your kids when they ask for things (I know I am!) and congratulate and encourage the girls in your life when you see them asking.

5. ASK ASK ASK! Ask for a raise, negotiate contracts, and don't discount your pricing. Sounds simple, but one of the key reasons women make less is because we don't ask for more. Let's take a page from the guys on this one, shall we?

Conclusion: Pulling It All Together

————————◆————————

You now know five strategies that can really accelerate things for you, and I've outlined 25 Power Moves for you to make them come alive. How are you doing? Are you taking time to complete or implement the Power Moves? You're done reading the second book, and I really want to hear about your wins! Send me an email or join in the conversation on my blog:

Mo@moxieexchange.com

www.moxieexchange.com/blog

The results you get from this book are only going to be as good as the action you take and the ideas you choose to execute on. Take ACTION. In the next book, *5 Beliefs of Winning Women*, I share 5 beliefs that really successful women hold, most of which will surprise you. Keep working your way through the *Rock Your Moxie: Power Moves for Women Leading the Way* series and don't forget to check in with me along the way. I'd also love for you to be a part of the Rock Your Moxie: A Monthly Shot of Leadership & Success community where I lead a monthly online workshop covering the ideas and Power Moves from the books. There's no cost to attend the workshop (remember that part about needing

YOU at the table?) and it will really make the content come to life for you. Plus, you're bound to connect with some very interesting and successful women who are getting after it like you.

Go, Girl! Get out there and hit the gas on your success!

The 25 Power Moves

Live on the Skinny Branches

1. Pick a decision you've found yourself holding back on and playing it safe about, and create a 'worst case scenario' chart to help you move forward. At the top, write down the decision, with three columns below it. In column 1, write down the worst case scenario, in column 2, how you'll know you've gotten there/indicators you have reached the worst case, in column 3 what action you will take.

2. Host a lunch/happy hour in honor of your biggest screw up. Own, celebrate, laugh at and discuss when things didn't go as planned. Share what you learned and how the 'failure' has helped move you forward.

3. Name your fears and talk them down. "If I do x I'm afraid that y will happen."

4. Do a debrief on the things you're initially categorizing as a 'failure'. Answer these questions: What went right? What did I learn? How did I just fail forward toward success?

5. Have a fan club. Yes, a fan club. Have a few key people from your inner circle that you have set up an explicit arrangement with in advance so they understand their role. When you are feeling fearful or worried about failing,

call them up or meet with them to say, "This is scaring the crap out of me!" or, "I'm about to go really, really big on this one." Their job is to tell you that you are a brilliant rock star, you've got this, and that they are holding the safety net for you. They are not there to go through contingency plans, or cost benefit analysis. They are there to push your butt out on the skinny branch and cheer you on. Trust me, it works.

Suck It Up and Shake It Off

1. Take all your gripes, complaints, slights, bad blood, excuses, health issues etc and write them on individual slips of paper. Really purge. Get it all out. Place them in a fireplace or fireproof container (old coffee cans work great), light a match, drop it in, burn the hell out of them and ceremonially LET THEM GO. I've done this with everyone from highly successful executives to teenagers and every time it's pure magic.

2. Tune in to the conversations you are a part of. You're going to be amazed how much victim talk surrounds you. Make a vow to not chime in when excuses, blame or complaints come up. Either change the conversation or walk away.

3. When you feel the urge to throw a pity party bubbling up, ask yourself these three questions: "This is hard compared to *what*?" "Is anyone going to die?" "What am I supposed to

learn from this?"

4. When you find yourself replaying a failure, literally tell yourself, "Stop! We've moved on from that." Refocus by rewriting a goal you are working on. Determine two clear action items, that you can complete by the end of the day, toward accomplishing that goal.

5. Create visual prompts or mental cues to remind yourself to suck it up and shake it off. Photos, screen savers, and vivid memories that you can draw up quickly all work well.

Pay To Play

1. Add a 'learning and growth' line to your budget. You should be spending at least as much annually on your professional and leadership learning and development as you are on your 'external' brand (clothes, shoes, hair, makeup, jewelry.) The money IS there. It's about making the choice on where you're going to spend it.

2. Subscribe to a few good magazines or blogs that are focused on leadership and success. You'll learn from their content and also find out about good programs and resources by what they are covering.

3. Poll successful women in your life about places they go for learning and growth. Ask them what organizations, programs and resources have contributed to their growth and success.

4. Commit 30 minutes a day to learning. Block it in your calendar.

5. Start a learning library. Start building up books, audios etc that have been recommended to you as growth building blocks.

Get Your Happy On

1. Wake up every day and choose happiness and joy. If you get off track, remember that you can choose again. Create joy in your world.

2. Pick one thing to keep with you that is guaranteed to make you smile. I used to carry a small picture of my husband's high school graduation photo with me (he was wearing a blue velvet tux) and would pull it out when I needed a lift.

3. Get really interested in other people and tuned in to their emotions, especially the people closest to you. Figure out the things that you do consistently and authentically that make you and other people feel good. Do more of them.

4. Choose your news media carefully. Sensationalism and fear sell, so that's what the news is loaded with. Watching it has a big impact on your well- being. Consider skimming only headlines from a few different sources.

5. Build some silliness into your life. For example, on Friday mornings I hold what is know in our household as 'Friday morning dance party.' I turn on bad 80's music and shake

my bootie all around the kitchen. My teenagers, who are wiped out by that point of the week truly *cannot* stop themselves from laughing and I feel great, too.

Ask Until Your Knees Shake

1. Change your mindset and start to think about just about everything as negotiable. You'll be amazed at what's possible. Babcock suggests starting small, and practicing. Ask the cleaners to have your clothes ready a day earlier, ask if there's a fresher cut of fish at the market, ask for an even lower rate at the hotel and an even later check-out.

2. Become a master negotiator. Set a goal for yourself to become an expert (or at least proficient) on negotiations. Take a class. Read up on negotiation skills and practice, practice, practice.

3. Share the research and results with your daughters and colleagues. Mentor young women on how to ask and negotiate.

4. Watch how you're responding to your kids when they ask for things (I know I am!) and congratulate and encourage the girls in your life when you see them asking.

5. ASK ASK ASK! Ask for a raise, negotiate contracts, and don't discount your pricing. Sounds simple, but one of

the key reasons women make less is because we don't ask for more. Let's take a page from the guys on this one, shall we?

Rock *your* *Moxie*

Power Moves for Women Leading the Way

5 Beliefs *of* Winning Women

by Maureen Berkner Boyt

Rock Your Moxie:

Power Moves for Women Leading the Way

5 Beliefs of Winning Women

Maureen Berkner Boyt

Table of Contents

Click here to join a community of women in an online monthly workshop covering ideas and Power Moves from the book

Chapter 1 Women Are a Sisterhood

Last year I spent a week with an extraordinary group of businesswomen in South Florida and Atlanta. These women bestowed innovative ideas, intelligent thinking, laughter, and moxie upon one another. Businesses moved forward because of their interactions. And yet, at the end of one evening the "women don't support one another" conversation came up. The tired 'women stab each other in the back' type statements were made.

ENOUGH! STOP DRINKING THAT KOOL-AID!

I'm only going to say this 1,000 times, really. We have got to STOP perpetuating the myth that women in the workplace don't support one another. Enough already! It's total bullshit, and we really don't need the next generation believing, and thus expecting, that women are out to get them on the job. For that matter, we don't need the generations at work right now spending the mental energy and resources grinding their teeth about a legacy issue when there are WAY bigger and less mythical fish to fry! Excuse the strong language, but I am weary of the serious damage done to women by this seemingly innocuous conversation.

Women at the top of their game know the real deal, and

believe that women are a strong, supportive sisterhood.

No, this group is not a tribe of Pollyannas. They know there are some tough people in this world who will step on you as soon as spit in your eye, and all behind your back. They also understand that's not a skill set limited to the female population. They don't pull out the bad experiences they've had with women and make those exceptions to the rule the gospel truth.

Yes, everyone has a story about a woman who was evil to her at work. Guess what? Everyone has a story about a man who was evil to them at work, too. This isn't a gender issue; it's an emotional intelligence issue. I recently read an article in an online business journal that got my blood boiling with the title, "Mean Girl Syndrome in the Workplace." Really? Is this 6th grade? Some of the language in the article included 'back stabbing'. I had to reply. Here is an excerpt of my comments on the article:

> *"The poor interactions I've been a part of came down to one of us (male/female) not behaving in an emotionally intelligent manner. Think back over your last 100 interactions with women- I would hazard that 100 of them were positive, same as with men. Instead we focus on the 1/1,000 interaction we had with a woman that didn't go well and raise the flag that women are 'backstabbers', which*

we don't do when it's with a man. We are doing ourselves a disservice and undermining the wonderful support that women give and receive from one another every day. Let's stop making the exception the rule, stop using phrases like 'mean girl syndrome', and start focusing on..."

Start focusing on what? Start focusing on what highly successful women are paying attention to already: thinking bigger, asking for more, mentoring and sponsoring one another, raising our emotional intelligence, getting a woman in the White House, securing equal pay, getting more women in the C-Suite and on boards, the list goes on!

You see, looking around believing that half of the people in your professional sphere are not supportive is a ridiculously limiting belief. Really think about that. THAT'S the insidiousness of the 'women don't support' mantra. It subtly puts our guard up. Whether you recognize it or not, your subconscious mind is looking for reasons to prove out your belief. If you believe that women don't support one another, you throw up an unrecognized, unnecessary hurdle for another woman to jump before you will trust her." Hurdles slow you down.

The implications of how things stand today go further. Research by McKinsey shows that women already have to be performing at the next level to get a promotion while men only need to show the potential to perform in the job to get the same promotion. Not only have we set up a hurdle for women, it is set really, really high. The subtle, sinister belief that somehow we're out to get one another is slowing us all down.

Believe what winning women know to be true; women have got one another's backs. *People* have got one another's backs. The people in your world want you to succeed. The people around you are intelligent, thoughtful human beings who have ideas and resources to share with you. Wow, what a difference! Winning women now have 50% more of the population on their side, 50% more people to have meaningful connections with, learn from, be sponsored by, have on their teams... Is it any wonder that they are achieving high levels of success?

Enough with the drivel, then, about not supporting one another. Let's spend our time and energy on the evidence-backed issues that will really move the dial for women in the workplace and in the world. The next time you hear the old, worn, inaccurate soundtrack about women being evil to one another, speak up and stand for the truth. It will help all of us.

Chapter 1 Power Moves

1. Do the '20 interactions' exercise. Think back on the last 20 interactions you had with the women in your life. Were they positive or negative? Now think back on the last 20 interactions you had with the men in your life. Were they positive or negative?

2. Sit down with the girls in your life and share stories about women supporting one another. Step in when you hear them talking about girls being 'mean' or 'backstabbing' and let them know that after the teen years (where female social aggression is real), women are a supportive sisterhood.

3. Check on your biases. Are you expecting 'more' from women? Be particularly attuned to this during hiring, promotion, compensation, project assignment and vendor selection decisions.

4. Initiate conversations amongst women about this topic. Get proactive about changing the dialogue and clearing the hurdles for your and other women's success.

5. When you hear someone perpetuating the 'women don't support' myth, STEP UP and stop the conversation. Help re-frame the issue to emotional intelligence vs. gender.

Chapter 2 Wonder Woman Is a Fraud

I had a client who kept a Super Man doll that was still in its original packaging in a straight line of sight from his desk. When I asked him about it, he said that a client of his had given it to him after he'd made some heroic efforts to get a project finished for them. He kept it there to remind himself that he SHOULDN'T play Super Man. If he did, he was limiting his team's growth because they'd assume he'd always come in and 'save the day', and clients would always look to him, instead of his team, for answers. He'd also be stuck in the role, which he knew was unsustainable, because eventually his super-human 'strength' would fail him. What a brilliant reminder that solo efforts are almost never successful ones.

*What you will consistently hear from top performing women is that their growth really took off when they **stopped** trying to be Wonder Woman.*

I find it a bit ironic that there's a perception that men are bad at asking for help, and women are great at it. While that may be true in our personal lives, I've observed just the opposite to be true in the professional world. Women will get it done on their own or die trying. Better to gut it out than have anyone think we don't know it all or can't do it all. We have unrealistic expectations about what we should be able to do on our own, and it hurts us in the workplace. We slave away trying to figure something out, when that wheel has already been created.

Trying to do it all leads to burnout, mistakes and slow delivery. Yes, Ginger Rogers did everything Fred Astaire did in heels and backwards, but she also was focused just on the dancing, not on the show's production, hiring, lighting, ticket sales... You get my point.

Power women, though, have 'let go to grow.' They believe that asking for help is not a sign of weakness; it's a sign of emotional intelligence. They have a brilliant understanding of how to tap the energies and efforts of the people around them to enable high performance. They know their unique strengths and spend their time focused on those things and are master delegators of the rest. They don't try to be Wonder Woman; they build their own 'Justice League'.

Right now, the people around you have you well trained. I know that sounds harsh, but I didn't write this to make you feel warm and fuzzy. I wrote this to help you get out of your own way and succeed at higher levels. Your team and your family know they can come to you and you will have the answer or will respond with something like, "Just give it to me and I'll take care of it." You're a superhero in your own mind, when in fact they have the power to make you jump.

You've got to believe that the people around you are capable, bright and have areas of expertise where they can run circles around you. Build growth momentum for yourself and your team through the power of questions. When someone comes to you for an answer instead of jumping right in with the solution, respond with, 'What do you think?' Then SHUT UP. This is going to take some self-control. They will likely respond with, 'I don't know', in the early days because you've always answered in the past! Respond with, 'If you did know, what would you think?' Again, SHUT UP. Wait for them to come up with an answer. They will, and it's probably going to be something good. Keep it up. You will be amazed how quickly the dialogue changes. I've had a saying that I've used for years that everybody understands and remembers: "If you bring me a dead cat, you must also bring me a shovel." Absolutely you can bring me problems or questions, but you must also come with a potential solution or answer.

Successful women build a team of people smarter than they are and know their team's solutions are almost always better than what they would have come up with one their own. There are going to be times when this is not the case, and the real magic is in how you handle those situations. You may have more experience, knowledge or context that shows you their next steps or solutions won't work. This is a perfect opportunity to coach. Share your decision making process: the factors you considered, the larger context of your past experience and so on. Resist the urge to take back over and say, 'Let me handle it.' Yes, you are going to have to commit some extra time in the early days as everyone learns this new way of operating. Think of it as going slow now so youcan go really fast later. You are building the capabilities of your team, freeing you up to take on the next big opportunity.

I hereby ask each one of the over-achieving-thanks-I-can-get-it-I-should-be-smart-enough-talented-enough-faster-better-stronger women reading this to DITCH YOUR WONDER WOMAN LASSO. It's time. Ask for help. Collaborate. Get someone else to do it. Realize when something is 'good enough' and stop there. Delegate. If you don't those super human efforts will eventually come back to harm you, whether it be in compromised health or relationships or in limited opportunities, because being Wonder Woman has its limits!

Chapter 2 Power Moves

1. Learn to be an *effective* delegator. This means setting everyone up for success. You need to be explicit about

expectations of results, timelines, and levels of decision-making authority. Know that your team may do something differently than you would have, but that the end result is what is important.

2. Share with your team that you have set a goal to be a better delegator and create a stronger team. Ask them to call you on it when they see you acting like Wonder Woman. Add an item to your team meeting agenda where the team will quickly grade your delegation effectiveness and give you suggestions for improvement.

3. Use the power of questions to elicit the best from your team and family. Here are some good questions to start with: What do you think we should do? What ideas do you have? What do you think the next step should be? How would you handle it?

4. Ask for help in your personal life. You should not be the only one taking care of the house, shopping etc. If your family is unwilling or inconsistently stepping up, get a new family. Joking! Pay someone. Your time is far too valuable to spend cleaning toilets. If you're worried about the money, ask that this be the gift you get for your birthday

and the holidays.

5. Be kind to yourself. Guilt is self-limiting. There is always going to be someone that you think 'has it all together' who is bringing a 3-tiered cake to your kid's soccer game when you brought the pre-made Rice Krispie treats. You are doing the best you can, and it is enough. You're the only one who compares and cares.

Chapter 3 I'm Ready

A male friend of mine who is almost ten years younger than me and is self-taught in his industry recently shared that he'd been in negotiations to take over the CEO role of a large, growing company. He was confident that he could make significant positive changes and was uniquely qualified for the role. In the end he had decided not to take the position because it didn't fit with his long-range goals. I had to laugh. I had also been approached recently about a CEO role. My initial response was very different from my friend's confident air though. It was a knee-jerk, "I'm not qualified." It took me about 30 seconds before I slapped myself upside the head and thought, "Of course I'm qualified. Of course they would ask me."

That wasn't my first response though. I first went to the place of assessing all of the reasons why I was NOT ready for the role. My friend's initial response was, 'These guys would be lucky to have me.' Our backgrounds are very similar, though I have the added edge of 10 years more experience and an advanced degree. Yet, I was the one initially doubting my readiness for a similar opportunity!

What is important is that I quickly did get to the place of

believing I was ready, qualified and deserving. *These are key beliefs of powerful women.*

My original response, self-doubt, is not an unusual one for women. When sharing the experience and my re-framing with several women, they had all experienced the same thing. We set our own bar extraordinarily high and question our readiness for opportunities, whether that's landing a huge client or the next level promotion. The hiring managers I know share story after story of women not even throwing their hats in the ring for opportunities because they don't think they're qualified. Some great on-going research shows that men take job requirements as suggestions, women as hard and fast qualifiers. We'll look at the same job description and the woman will see 10 things she's done and two that she hasn't and not apply. A man will see the same description and think,' I've done six of those, and know I can figure out the other four. I'm going to apply and ask for top dollar.'

There are plenty of messages feeding this belief that women are less qualified, too. If you pay attention to who is quoted on the topics of business, success and leadership, 95% of them are men. Last October, the latest version of Success Magazine came in the mail. My daughter saw it on the counter and said, "What a surprise. Another man on the cover." Ouch! Let's not even get into the gender stereotypes and objectification of women in the media that surround us everywhere we go.

You need to be able to step past all of this though, and know that you are ready and qualified for what is next. You do not need to have every answer. You do not need to have already been successful at something to step into that something! That's called gaining expertise. You need to know that you have the skills and potential to get there.

Pay attention to the understated messages telling you you're not ready, and don't buy in. An e-newsletter landed in my inbox a few weeks ago with details about the latest 'board readiness' program for women. I find programs like this both ridiculous and insulting. When is the last time, if ever, you've seen the same program advertised for men? What these programs imply is that somehow professional women are less able and ready to step into board of directors positions than men. That we need to prepped and tweaked and found up to snuff and THEN we're ready for prime time. The guys however? They're good to go as is. Please spare me the flawed thinking.

Serving on boards is a big-damned deal. It's where the power plays are made, and you should be setting your sights on getting your well-qualified butt in one of those chairs. In the past there was always conversation about women not having the experience that men do and thus not being as qualified. I'm calling bullshit. Look at the latest stats about women and MBA's, women and accounting degrees, and how we outpace men in graduation rates from high school, college and advanced degrees. What needs to change is the unfounded bias that somehow, because we're women , we're just not "ready".

Business is not rocket science. Reading financial statements is not akin to decoding the Rosetta Stone. You need to understand fundamental principles about market drivers, cash, talent management and the like. Most importantly, you need to be able to understand and 'see' the game and anticipate what's next. You need the ability to understand the long-range implications of decisions and a sense of when to act quickly and when to hold. That has nothing to do with what's between your legs and everything to do with what's between your ears. Oh, but you say, 'women haven't been in financial roles in big companies.' That's like saying anyone who hasn't given birth shouldn't be a parent. There's a hell of a lot more to parenting than childbirth, and there's a hell of a lot more to making strategic decisions for a company than having prepared the financial statements.

I'd pay attention if someone put on a program for women called 'board positioning'. The training would be about understanding that you ARE ready and taking the steps to ensure you are a candidate when board positions open up. It would be designed to show the ins and outs of the back room jockeying / golf course conversations that takes place as board positions open up and how to be sure your name was thrown in the ring. It would be about revealing the gaps in the relationships you have that open boardroom doors and how to meet and connect with those people in a meaningful way. Now THAT kind of training we could use!

Are you ready? Of course you are. Just make sure you believe it.

Chapter 3 Power Moves

1. Keep an accomplishments list or portfolio of your work that you can easily access to remind yourself what you are capable of.

2. If you're in a position to hire or select vendors, understand that qualified women may not be stepping up. Seek out women you believe are qualified and ask them to consider applying or pursuing the work. Sometimes a nudge is all it takes.

3. Change your mindset from 'already performing' to 'able to grow into' when looking at potential opportunities.

4. Take requirements as suggestions. Go for that big client, pursue the promotion, ask for the stretch assignment.

5. Catch yourself when you find yourself short-changing your abilities and questioning your qualifications and change your internal dialogue to, "I'm ready and I'm qualified." If that's not enough, think of a person you know that you are most shocked to find out has been very successful (I have a few stoners I knew in high school I think about in these situations) and remind yourself that if they can do it, you sure as hell can, too. Do the same for other women if you hear them downplaying their work or abilities.

Chapter 4 Bring Your "A" Game

A friend and former client of mine once said, "Perfection is not a reasonable expectation. Excellence is." That perfectly articulates a key belief of high performers. *Always aim for excellence, and don't let the fallacy of perfection slow you down.*

But there's more. *Women who really have it going on don't aim for excellence in everything.* They pick a few strengths and key gamer-changers and aim for excellence and mastery in those areas. The rest? They let it go. They either delegate or are okay with being average.

We've built up myths of the perfect job, the perfect family, the perfect team. They just don't exist. Trying to do something 'perfectly' leads to frustration and wasted time. It's like being on a quest for the unattainable. I started out my work life in the print business and I will never, ever forget the day I walked into the pre-press department and overheard and watched one of my co-workers, who was on the phone with a client working on a photo for their clothing catalog. "Oh, so you want her boobs to look a little rounder? Like they're actually coming up out of her top? Got it." Click, click, click went his mouse and up, up, up went her boobs. Poof. The myth of a perfect body disappeared before my eyes. It was freeing. So is the overall idea that perfection is not a reasonable expectation.

Excellence is another matter. Believing that excellence is attainable, and aiming for excellence is the hallmark of high performers. Wanting to bring your "A" game and pursuing excellence is about being on a continual quest to get better, to know more, to be more capable, to work toward mastery. That's heady stuff.

I went to the symphony a few weeks ago and was swept away by excellence. In particular, there were three people whose performances took my breath away: the Conductor, the Concertmaster and the guest pianist. I wish you could have seen them at work- they were vibrant, present, completely committed to excellence in what they were creating. Watching them was electrifying and inspiring. I knew they had gotten to this moment and this performance by the pursuit of excellence.

When you talk with women leading the way, this belief bubbles to the surface almost immediately. Kim Jordan, the CEO of New Belgium Brewing talks about beer making as an ancient craft and how they continue to hone that craft at New Belgium. Colleen Abdoulah, Chairwoman and CEO at WOW! talks about continually working towards creating a customer experience that lives up to the company name. They are both deeply committed to excellence. The beautiful thing about this is how much we grow as individuals as we pursue excellence. If I want to do something better, I need to become better. It means that what constitutes our "A" game continues to shift upward. What was excellence last year is now our average performance.

We need to re-commit to excellence, to bringing our "A" game, all the time. The truth is, it's really easy to fall into the trap of "good enough" or even "better than average." It seems there's a conspiracy of mediocrity these days. Good really IS the enemy of great. It can be easy to get sloppy. Ninotchka Rosca first coined the term "crab mentality" for situations where people attempt to "pull down" anyone who starts to achieve success beyond the others. Sometimes the "good enough" trap can feel like "stay still" or "be satisfied." When you are pursuing excellence, none of those options are acceptable.

Think about walking into every day like you are about to perform a Beethoven symphony. You want to end each day knowing that in at least some small way, you pursued excellence. Maybe it was in a phone call, an email or a conversation with your kids. Perhaps you learned a new fact or a technique that will improve upon what you're doing even slightly. Even if you miss the mark sometimes, your performance will be better for having tried.

Chapter 4 Power Moves

1. Take some time with this one. Determine what you want to become masterful at. What are those few things that are worthy of your pursuit of excellence?

2. Build the question, "What did I do this week to pursue excellence?" into your habits and routines.

3. Make sure your team understands the pursuit of excellence and the fallacy of perfection. Have a meeting to discuss the idea that "Perfection is an unrealistic expectation, excellence is not," and what that looks like for your team.

4. Go see a master at work. It might be a performer, a speaker, an athlete or an artist. Watch someone who has pursued excellence in their craft or career to the level of mastery.

5. Kick a few things off your list. Intentionally let a few small things slip through the cracks.

Chapter 5 Impatience Is a Virtue

From a very young age I remember my mom telling me, "Maureen, patience is not your virtue." That used to sting, but now I'm glad I'm wired for speed and action. I'd like to see more women feeling impatient at work and in life. Waiting patiently to be noticed for nailing our projects, or for the raise, or the board of directors seat, or the promotion, or the _____ (fill in the blank on the thing you're waiting for) is kicking women's teeth in. A little impatience would go a long, long way toward progress.

I'm not suggesting women get pushy or disrespectful. Those are career killers. I *am* suggesting you get impatient about how much money you're making, how far up the food chain you are, the size of the client deals you are landing, the quality of the projects you're assigned and the like. Is your company growing fast enough for you? I hope not. Are you satisfied with the status quo? Horrifying thought, isn't it?

Once you're feeling impatient, you take action. Once you've got the itch that something has to change, or that things need to move faster, or that an idea's time has come, it's almost impossible to sit back as a spectator in your own world. You've got to move! You become the star in your own action movie.

Successful women don't wait for opportunity to come their way, or to be recognized for their efforts. *They believe it is okay to take action to move the dial for themselves. They believe in making their own luck.*

I'm not saying we should run around being impatient about everything. People, emotions and relationships all require patience. If I rush a relationship before I've built trust, I kill any hope of that trust developing. It feels like I'm trying to get to something through you instead of creating an opportunity with you. If I'm strong-arming you through a process, it feels like just that. I have to respect your space and pace, too. You've got to have enough track record or data to stake a claim.

I've got the scars to show from when I've jumped too fast and the parachute wasn't even on my back yet. however, I have far more experiences where my impatience served me well. Hell, I started The Moxie Exchange Movement because I got impatient waiting for someone else to start a group where I could be around ridiculously brilliant professional women taking action who were as wired for growth as I am. I couldn't WAIT any longer- it was time to MOVE. It's times like that that you should grab the steering wheel, hit the gas, and make things happen.

Don't be patient with your own growth and don't be patient with pursuing opportunities. Actively pursue the big deal, promotion or spotlight opportunity. There's never going to be a right time and the 'perfect' next step doesn't exist. Figure out how to grab a new skill set. Go after that opportunity. Do NOT be patient. Get your impatience on and GET AFTER IT. Be impatient about shaping your destiny. Be your own pace car, and push the envelope on the speed you set. Be impatient in pursuing your ambitions. Yes, ambitions. That is not a dirty word, sister. I hope you have huge, huge ambitions and that you are impatiently pursuing them.

Rear Admiral Grace Hopper's statement, "It's easier to ask forgiveness than it is to get permission", is one of the truest proclamations ever spoken. If you're waiting patiently for permission, the parade of men asking for more money, a promotion, a better interest rate etc., will pass you by. You're going to be the one cleaning up the horse crap and ticker tape. Stop waiting. Start doing. Get impatient with how things are, and start taking action. Let impatience be your virtue!

Chapter 5 Power Moves

1. What small things are you disgusted with in your life? What are you pissed off about? I don't care if it's your ugly curtains or the nose whistle emanating from the guy in the office next to you. Stop patiently waiting for those things to change. Determine three clear action steps to change them,

starting TODAY. Starting with the small things will get the ball rolling for you. It's also going to clear up head-space for you to focus on the big things.

2. Go bigger. What are the next level things on your list of 'this just isn't working?' Again, create a plan and do one thing a day to achieve it.

3. What are your ambitions? What are the big plans you have for yourself that you may not have even said aloud to anyone? Stop waiting. Start moving.

4. Identify the *One Thing* that could change everything for you. Think of it as a catalyst, an accelerator, that if it happens things REALLY start moving for you. Is it landing the showcase client? Booking the prime time interview? Being picked up by the trade journal? It's going to feel audacious when you figure it out.

5. Stop waiting for your game-changer One Thing to magically 'transpire'. Fairy tales feature wimpy women and you don't fit that mold. I want you to make a very specific plan to make it happen. Do your research. Create a budget if it needs one. Make this sucker real. Impatiently execute on that plan like your ambition depends upon it, because it does. Go, Go, GO!!

Conclusion: Pulling It All Together

A big part of success is getting out of your own way, and that really is evident in the five beliefs I've outlined here. I'll keep saying this: you've already got what it takes to be as successful as you want. You simply need to believe it and keep doing the things that high performers do at the next level and the next level and the next. You've got it going on or you wouldn't be reading books like this. Keep pushing the envelope on what's possible for yourself. The fourth book, _5 Ways Influential Women Sustain Their Edge_ is about how you sustain your moxie as you grow. Pushing for 'more' can lead to flinging yourself out of orbit if you're not careful! The practices I outline in the next book ensure you stay 'grounded' during your upward trajectory.

Shoot me an email _Mo@moxieexchange.com_ and let me know how you are progressing or share ideas you use to rock your moxie. I'm going to start sharing some insider resources on my blog _www.moxieexchange.com/blog_ so make sure you've joined the tribe online. If you have not joined the conversation happening in the Rock Your Moxie: A Monthly Shot of Leadership & Success community, I'd really love to see you jump in. Every month I lead an online workshop covering the ideas and Power Moves from the books and there's no cost to attend. Plus, you're bound to connect with some very interesting and successful women who are getting after it like you.

Believe BIG, my friend!

The 25 Power Moves

Women Are A Sisterhood

1. Do the '20 interactions' exercise. Think back on the last 20 interactions you had with the women in your life. Were they positive of negative? Now think back on the last 20 interactions you had with the men in your life. Were they positive or negative?

2. Sit down with the girls in your life and share stories about women supporting one another. Step in when you hear them talking about girls being 'mean' or 'backstabbing' and let them know that after the teen years (where female social aggression is real), women are a supportive sisterhood.

3. Check on your biases. Are you expecting 'more' from women? Be particularly attuned to this during hiring, promotion, compensation, project assignment and vendor selection decisions.

4. Initiate conversations amongst women about this topic. Get proactive about changing the dialogue and clearing the hurdles for your and other women's success.

5. When you hear someone perpetuating the 'women don't support' myth, STEP UP and stop the conversation. Help

re-frame the issue to emotional intelligence vs. gender.

Wonder Woman Is A Fraud

1. Learn to be an *effective* delegator. This means setting everyone up for success. You need to be explicit about expectations of results, timelines, and levels of decision-making authority. Know that your team may do something differently than you would have, but that the end result is what is important.

2. Share with your team that you have set a goal to be a better delegator and create a stronger team. Ask them to call you on it when they see you acting like Wonder Woman. Add an item to your team meeting agenda where the team will quickly grade your delegation effectiveness and give you suggestions for improvement.

3. Use the power of questions to elicit the best from your team and family. Here are some good questions to start with: What do you think we should do? What ideas do you have? What do you think the next step should be? How would you handle it?

4. Ask for help in your personal life. You should not be the only one taking care of the house, shopping etc. If your family is unwilling or inconsistently stepping up, get a new family. Joking! Pay someone. Your time is far too valuable to spend cleaning toilets. If you're worried about the

money, ask that this be the gift you get for your birthday and the holidays.

5. Be kind to yourself. Guilt is self-limiting. There is always going to be someone that you think 'has it all together' who is bringing a 3-tiered cake to your kid's soccer game when you brought the pre-made Rice Krispie treats. You are doing the best you can, and it is enough. You're the only one who compares and cares.

I'm Ready

1. Keep an accomplishments list or portfolio of your work that you can easily access to remind yourself what you are capable of.
2. If you're in a position to hire or select vendors, understand that qualified women may not be stepping up. Seek out women you believe are qualified and ask them to consider applying or pursuing the work. Sometimes a nudge is all it takes.
3. Change your mindset from 'already performing' to 'able to grow into' when looking at potential opportunities.
4. Take requirements as suggestions. Go for that big client, pursue the promotion, ask for the stretch assignment.
5. Catch yourself when you find yourself short-changing your abilities and questioning your qualifications and change your internal dialogue to, "I'm ready and I'm qualified." If

that's not enough, think of a person you know that you are most shocked to find out has been very successful (I have a few stoners I knew in high school I think about in these situations) and remind yourself that if they can do it, you sure as hell can, too. Do the same for other women if you hear them downplaying their work or abilities.

Bring Your "A" Game

1. Take some time with this one. Determine what you want to become masterful at. What are those few things that are worthy of your pursuit of excellence?

2. Build the question, 'What did I do this week to pursue excellence?' into your habits and routines.

3. Make sure your team understands the pursuit of excellence and the fallacy of perfection. Have a meeting to discus what "perfection is an unrealistic expectation, excellence is not" looks like for your team.

4. Go see a master at work. It might be a performer, a speaker, an athlete or an artist. Watch someone who has pursued excellence in their craft or career to the level of mastery.

5. Kick a few things off your list. Intentionally let a few small things slip through the cracks.

Let Impatience Be Your Virtue

1. What small things are you disgusted with in your life? What are you pissed off about? I don't care if it's your ugly curtains or the nose whistle emanating from the guy in the office next to you. Stop patiently waiting for those things to change. Determine three clear action steps to change them, starting TODAY. Starting with the small things will get the ball rolling for you. It's also going to clear up head-space for you to focus on the big things.

2. Go bigger. What are the next level things on your list of 'this just isn't working?' Again, create a plan and do one thing a day to achieve it.

3. What are your ambitions? What are the big plans you have for yourself that you may not have even said aloud to anyone? Stop waiting. Start moving.

4. Identify the *One Thing* that could change everything for you. Think of it as a catalyst, an accelerator, that if it happens things REALLY start moving for you. Is it landing the showcase client? Booking the prime time interview? Being picked up by the trade journal? It's going to feel audacious when you figure it out.

5. Stop waiting for your game-changer One Thing to magically 'transpire'. Fairy tales feature wimpy women and you don't fit that mold. I want you to make a very specific plan to make it happen. Do your research. Create a

budget if it needs one. Make this sucker real. Impatiently execute on that plan like your ambition depends upon it, because it does. Go, Go, GO!!

No 4

Rock your *Moxie*

Power Moves for Women Leading the Way

5 Ways Influential Women Sustain Their Edge

by Maureen Berkner Boyt

Rock Your Moxie:

Power Moves for Women Leading the Way

5 Ways Influential Women Sustain Their Edge

Maureen Berkner Boyt

Table of Contents

<u>Click here to join a community of women in an online monthly workshop covering ideas and Power Moves from the book</u>

Chapter 1 Gratitude with a Side of "More"

Mary Coombs is a woman with an attitude. She built and sold a large, successful marketing agency, which when she was at the helm worked with clients like Duke Energy, Eastman Kodak and Bayer. They racked up industry awards. She's been married to the same great guy for 30 plus years and they have two great daughters. She lives on a lake and they have dinner parties with great friends on the weekends. A rosy picture, yes? There's more to Mary's story. She doesn't come from wealth and worked her butt off for years to get her business off the ground, one of her daughters is wheelchair bound as a result of Spina Bifida and Mary had her own tango with breast cancer a few years back. Any one of those things would be a showstopper for average performers. Three big reasons why life has given them the shaft, three big excuses for their results in life. Not Coombs. She has the perfect attitude combination, a combination that I see time and again in successful women like her. She's ridiculously grateful for all she has, while still wanting to see what more she can achieve. She doesn't dwell in the bad or rest on the laurels of what she's accomplished. She frequently shares that she's fortunate for all she has and in the next sentence will reveal six new things she's learning or taking on so she can be 'more' as a person.

Successful women hold a perfect tension between being

grateful for what they have and wanting more for themselves at the same time.

Understanding and appreciating what you have grounds you. Most people take for granted their health and that their most basic needs are met every day. Think about it. In the morning, do you turn off the alarm, hop out of bed, go to the bathroom, brush your teeth, grab some coffee, a bagel and a yogurt, and fire up your laptop (or something close to that routine)? In those few minutes alone you have over 15 things to be grateful for: you are in a home, you do not have to fear for your or your family's safety, your house has heat, a roof, electricity, and indoor plumbing. You have safe water to drink and easy access to healthy food. You have access to technology and unlimited information. You have the mental capabilities to make decisions. You can see, smell, hear, taste, walk and take care of your own basic physical needs without assistance. I could easily keep going, and I haven't even gotten past the first 15 minutes of your day or the bottom rungs of Maslow's hierarchy of needs! These needs are not commonly met around the world, and high achieving women always have that in mind and practice gratitude for what they have.

It's fun and informative to ask people how they build gratitude into their personal and business routines. A high tech CEO I worked with kept a small notebook with her that she'd jot gratitude thoughts in throughout her day as they occurred to her. Another woman I know keeps an Excel spread sheet (yes, she is a CPA) and friend's family keeps a 'gratitude jar' that they'll throw slips of paper or small things that represent what they're grateful for into. A company I worked with had a 'Gratitude Wall' where anyone could put up a sticky note with things they were grateful for, from the new coffee in the kitchen to the co-worker who saved their butt on a project.

I start my day with gratitude. Before my feet hit the floor I take a few quiet minutes and run through what I'm grateful for, always starting with, "I'm thankful for my strong and healthy body and my strong and healthy mind." I then run through a list of things I'm feeling grateful for that day. Sometimes it's a challenge I'm facing, because as Jim Rohn used to say, "Don't wish it was easier; wish you were better. Don't wish for less problems; wish for more skills. Don't wish for less challenges; wish for more wisdom." I'll include people on my list who bring me joy, or challenge my thinking or make me laugh- it all depends on the day. When I walk into the day filled with gratitude for what I have, I feel pretty invincible. Not a lot can get me down when I'm focused on what I have, not what I don't.

From a professional standpoint, spending time in gratitude is one of the most powerful habits you can adopt for yourself as a businesswoman. Don't go all Pollyanna on me and ignore the things that need fixing, but don't dwell there, and certainly don't have the reputation as the whiny kid down the block out in the marketplace. We've all done business with them (not for long) and it's less than pleasant. Focus and be thankful for what's going right, and plan on integrating that gratitude into how clients and influential people in your market experience you and your company.

You can't stop with gratitude, though. *Remember the edge comes from the tension between being grateful, AND wanting more.*

Things can get a little slippery here. If you're doing a great job focusing on and being grateful for all that you DO have, it can become a siren's song of "I have enough." I say siren's song, because HAVING enough is not what we're talking about here. Stuff is just stuff and more of it, in my opinion, brings more stress, not less. If you want more money or greater levels of success because you want more 'stuff', you're smoking something, and when you come down from the high, you're going to have a ripping headache and a lot of trinkets.

Rather, we're talking about LEARNING, ACHIEVING and BECOMING more. When that's what you're seeking, money and success will follow as a result of what you now know and are capable of. You're seeking a bigger and better "more" version of yourself. Cool, and worth the effort. As far as we know, we've got one spin around the big blue marble. Why not see how much MORE you can become? Why not go for it? That's the performance edge of high achievers. They're on an on-going quest to see just how much they can learn, become and be.

Chapter 1 Power Moves

1. Start a gratitude practice. Every day, name at least 5 things you are grateful for. If you already practice gratitude, up the ante and find a way to include your family, co-workers or close friends in your practice.

2. Share your gratitude freely. "I am so grateful to have you in my life." Or "I am so grateful for the opportunity you gave me." Or "I am so grateful for the x,y,z you bring to the team." Or any version of some genuine statement and sentiment like those is extraordinarily powerful and is a wonderful gift to give the people in your life.

3. Ask people how they express their gratitude at work, and personally. You'll hear all kinds of cool ideas you can adopt for your company or your own gratitude routine.

4. Set your 'more' thermostat to high. Why *not* see how much

you can learn and become? Get really comfortable with the idea. After you're comfortable, get really FIRED UP about the idea!

5. Read about some interesting, successful women who fit your definition of 'more'. How did they do it? What are lessons and ideas you can take from their 'more' excursions?

Chapter 2 Assume Good Intentions

Early in my career, I worked for a large printing company and was just hitting my stride in a department I'd been transferred to a few months prior. Every Thursday at 2:00pm, there was a massive deadline for shipping out a major national magazine, and my boss and I were the linchpins in making that happen in our department. From 9:30 am– 2:00 pm it was really crunch time. On a particular Thursday, my boss came in, checked in with me, and vanished. Gone. No response to pages, emails or inquiries about his whereabouts. As the morning progressed, I became more and more panicked as I dug into the work. By noon I was in a mental lather and working my butt off to meet the impending deadline. By 2:00 the work was done and I was PISSED. When my boss came into view about 15 minutes later, whistling no less, I lost my cool. I was young, and in those days had not yet learned to harness what has been referred to as 'my red-head temper.' I went off on him about how he'd taken off, leaving me to handle to work, how I was not his slave blah, blah, blah. Let's just say it was not one of my finer moments. A truly concerned and apologetic look passed over his face, and then he quietly said, "Maureen, I knew you could do it. I was giving you the chance to prove to yourself and the rest of the team that you've got what it takes and it's time for you to move on to the next challenge." Sigh. I had just fallen deep into the 'assuming bad intentions' trap and had turned a huge opportunity into a huge blunder. And it had all occurred because of my flawed thinking and framing of the situation.

What a waste this type of thinking is! I've found that it's the very rare case indeed where someone truly intended something bad to happen. Mostly, people are stumbling along doing the best they can and wanting to do good things in the world, or at least do no harm. We need to change the script of the stories we create in our heads about why people do things. Right now, the scripts are overwhelmingly negative and the personal and professional costs are astronomical. We have entire industries that feed off the fear and bad intentions mindset of most of the population!

Life is a lot easier when you assume good intentions from the people around you. There is so much energy, time and money wasted because most people assume just the opposite; they presume BAD intentions. We jump straight to the worst-case scenario about why a series of events transpired or why a set of decisions were made. It HAD to be that they were out to screw me over, right? They wanted me to fail! They're trying to get my job/customer/parking space!

Not women who've got it going on though. They presume people are out to do good and spend their energy and thinking on forward-facing ideas and solutions. *They free up mental and emotional capacity that the rest of the world is spending on conspiracy or negative thinking to instead up their own game, and that gives them a mental edge.*

In fact, what Joanna Barsh and her team at McKinsey and Company found in their research about remarkable female leaders was that this group practiced positive framing. They consistently adopted a constructive view of their world. Even when tough things happen, successful women assume good things will come from it. How about that! I found in all my interviews and conversations with the most successful women I know that they all believe in the good in others and see them as a positive force to assist them in their journey, and will likewise act as the same for them.

Instead of being angry, suspicious and on edge, assuming good intentions allows you to approach your work and life with a sense of curiosity and joy. Everything from how you interpret the email in your in-box to how you react to getting cut off in traffic changes. It really is amazing! Making the shift is simple and profound. It also takes diligence. The media, our hard wiring, and the people around us are trying to pull us back in when we frame the world in a different way. Once you've made the shift though, it becomes easier and easier to stay in good intentions mode, and more obvious when you don't. It's a lot more fun on the sunny side of the street.

Chapter 2 Power Moves

1. Start re-training your brain in a hotbed of bad intention thinking;: driving in your car. The next time someone cuts you off, or drives 55 in the left-hand lane or swerves into your lane, pay attention to your thinking. Is the script in your head sounding something like, "That friggin' idiot! What in the hell were they thinking?" or other choice phrases? Do a re-frame right then and there. Change your script to something like, "Nobody wants to be in an accident. They must have a boatload going on, or didn't see me. I hope they get to wherever they're going safely." Keep at this exercise until this is your natural first reaction most of the time. There are still going to be the, "You've GOT to be kidding me!" moments, but you'll find they are far and few between, and that your re-framing in the car sets the stage for assuming good intentions everywhere else.

2. Set a goal to notice and acknowledge 3-5 people doing good things in the world each day. When your radar is up for the good stuff, you'll start to see that most people really

ARE out to do good versus cause harm.

3. Adopt, "Everyone is doing the best that they can," as a life mantra.

4. When the occasion does arise (and it will) that you come across someone from 'the dark side' who intentionally hosed you or someone else, respond with empathy. I tend to say something like this to myself, "They must really lead a crappy life to want to do something like that to someone else. I'm glad I'm not living in their world."

5. Remember that we judge ourselves by our intentions and others by their results. When you are questioning why someone did something that outwardly looks like they were up to no good, don't waste energy making up stories about it. You truly have no idea. If you are able, ask them! If you're not, presume their intentions were good, but the results were bad and move on.

Chapter 3 Use Premium Fuel

———————

Think of 20 people you consider to be the most successful people you know, men or women. Get a mental picture of each one of them, really see them in your mind's eye. Ok- how many of them do you picture and think, "Wow, they really need to take better care of themselves?" How many of them are overweight? How many of them are smokers? How many are heavy drinkers? I'm guessing zero, or in the rare case, one or two of the people.

The mental energy it takes to be way out there, stretching every capability you have is extraordinary, and if your physical body isn't up to carting your brain and stress around, you don't have a hope of maintaining your metal edge. I had you do the previous exercise because when you really start to pay attention, you'll find that highly successful people, particularly women, understand the fundamental tie between our physical well being and our level of success.

You've got to take care of yourself physically to play at the highest levels.

Being in good physical shape gives you an edge on a whole host of fronts. The mental energy most women spend on weight issues can instead be directed toward constructive things like professional growth, problem solving or idea generation. The energy that comes from being fit allows to you sustain a 'playing' pace that leaves others in the dust. There's no 'recovering' from last night's drinking or coughing jags to clear your lungs. These ideas are not mind-bending. It's as simple as when you're in good shape, you feel good. When you feel good, you can knock it out of the park.

And then, there's the credibility issue. I told you at the start of this series and this book that I wasn't going to blow smoke up your skirt, and this is a topic that I know is charged for a lot of women. I'm interested in your success and having you lead the way though, and that means facing all kinds of topics head-on. Here goes: if you are overweight, a smoker or a heavy drinker, the message you are sending is that you do not respect yourself. That message messes with your credibility in a big way. There's a lot of research out there to back this up, and like it or not there are stigmas attached to being in bad physical shape.

So you're up by three if you're taking care of yourself physically: you feel great, you can bring your "A" game for longer, and you're seen as credible by your counterparts. I know all of this from experience, because I've been on both sides of the good/bad physical shape fence. I know how great I feel now, and the edge it gives me over most people, and how crappy I felt then and how it was holding me back. I was a party girl for a long time and often started the day with a hangover. I used food as a stress-reducer and carried extra weight. I was an intermittent runner but usually went months at a time without real physical exercise. I spent a lot of time feeling 'blah' and a lot of mental energy beating myself up about my choices. When I looked at what I wanted to do with my life, I knew I needed to make some changes.

The shifts in thinking and behavior that I made are consistent with what I hear from high performing women. Here are a few of the basics: everything in moderation, love and respect the body that you have, food is fuel so only put premium in your tank, move your body every day, get enough sleep. Again, not rocket science but these small shifts can have a profound impact on physical well-being. They are about living a healthy lifestyle in support of your ambitions.

There's another small but powerful success practice that I urge you to embrace. *Spend quiet time simply sitting and listening to yourself every day.*

You are brilliant. Your subconscious mind is working toward helping you achieve your goals all the time, and is incredibly creative, intuitive and receptive to new ideas. Really successful women create time to listen to those quiet, powerful thoughts that are waiting to be heard. Most people are caught up in the cacophony of the day; go, go, go. Radio or TV on, blue tooth connected, email alerts pinging. We get so caught up with 'doing' that we don't take time to 'be' and to 'think'. Top achievers understand how important quiet time with their thoughts is, and make it a priority.

Sue Kochan is CEO of one of the fastest growing marketing firms in the nation, and she spends an hour meditating every day. Colleen Abdoulah, Chairwoman and CEO of WOW! spends a week in a silence retreat each year. They are the gold standards. My goal is 5 minutes a day and they are 5 of the most important minutes I spend. The clarity, ideas and focus that come from those five minutes has led to things that have literally changed my life. It was from those quiet minutes that the idea for The Moxie Exchange Movement went from just being an idea, to a plan, to a living, breathing leadership organization. I'm living in Spain with my family right now because I took the time to listen to my thoughts. These books are a result of an idea that germinated during my quiet time. Good stuff!

This is one of the success principles that I have found is the easiest to let slip. On my group coaching calls, almost all participants share that they have some version of this in their own lives and that it's been really powerful for them, but that they do it really inconsistently. I had the same experience until I found a way to build quiet time into the morning routine I already had in place. Since it became a part of that routine, it is rare that I don't take the time.

Your body is the vehicle that is carrying your genius, talent and ambitions. Make sure it's tuned well and that you're feeding it only premium fuel. Eat well, sleep well, get outside in the sunshine and fresh air and move your body. Take some quiet time. Treat your body with the respect that it, and you, deserve.

Chapter 3 Power Moves

1. Move your body for 30 minutes a day. No excuses. Note that I'm not suggesting you sign up for a premium gym membership, run a marathon or become a black belt. That's not realistic for most people. Just be sure you're physically moving for at least 30 minutes at a stretch. Walk, dance, do a free online yoga class- whatever floats your boat. I take a walk with my husband every day and get the triple bump of time to connect with him, time outdoors and exercise. It is fun to occasionally set a really big stretch goal for yourself on the physical front, too. I've done a few killer trail-running races and ultra team relays because I wanted to see if I could.

2. Schedule 5 minutes of quiet a day into your schedule. You'll have the best luck doing this consistently if you build it into a routine you already have in place. If you're already doing this, keep rocking it. If not, a good way to start is to simply focus on your breathing- what does it sound like and feel like coming in and out of your body? Unlike full meditation where you are trying to clear your mind, start listening to what thoughts are coming up. Don't judge or sort, just listen and follow it on to the next thought that comes up. You might want to have a pad of paper handy for right after your quiet time to capture some of the ideas that come up for you.

3. Uncover any flawed thinking you may have about your body. I remember it like it was yesterday when my friend Jeff accidentally bumped up against my butt in the 7th grade and said, "It's like Jell-O!" I spent the next 20 years believing I had a Jell-O butt, hating it, and wishing it were small and flat. It wasn't until I started loving and appreciating the body that I do have that I started LOVING having 'junk in the trunk' as we fondly say in my family. I was running the wrong script in my head. Love, appreciate, respect and take care of what you've got, sister. If you need to, get help for any addictions or psychological traumas

that are at the root of your beliefs and behaviors. You don't need to do this solo, and sometimes things are bigger than we can take on ourselves.

4. Adopt a life mantra of "I lead a healthy lifestyle." When you fully embrace this simple but powerful belief, it becomes harder and harder to shove those potato chips in your mouth or have that extra cocktail. Your mind and body start to protect themselves because those behaviors are NOT consistent with your lifestyle.

5. Shop the circumference of the grocery store where the healthy, fresh foods are found. Aim for 'nothing from a can, nothing from a box.'

Chapter 4 Get Out and Play

"All work and no play makes Jack a dull boy." Forget being dull; all work and no play makes for stale thinking and low energy, and that's a career killer. In the fantastic book *The Power of Full Engagement* by Loehr & Schwartz (I highly recommend you read it!) they share their research about how energy management and not time management is the key to sustained success. There is a tie in with the ideas from the last chapter about being in good physical shape, but in this case I'm talking about how to maintain high mental energy and fresh thinking.

Nobody I know has gotten their brilliant ideas when they are strung out and so utterly sick of what they're working on that they are thinking of quitting it all and becoming a sheep farmer. We've all known the people who are so one dimensional in their thinking and ideas that you can practically pull a string on their back to hear them regurgitate the same, tired way they are going about their work and life.

Really successful women know that to keep their edge and perform at their highest levels, they need to be multi-dimensional.

They feed their creative thinking and mental acuity by

getting out of the business world headspace and doing totally unrelated things that they love. One of my favorite questions to ask women in leadership positions is, "What do you do for fun?" I continue to be delighted and inspired by the answers. Here's a sampling: the head of a software consulting company who just achieved her sommelier designation, a partner at a major national accounting firm who is a raving lunatic baseball fan, the head of a physician's group who is on a roller derby team and participates in urban assault races.

When you're out of your work-mode and 'playing,' you have the chance to interact with people that have wildly diverse backgrounds, ideas and opinions, not just industry wonks. You're giving your brain a break from churning on the same information and letting your subconscious mind out to play. You're also collecting ideas. Tamara Kleinberg is the founder of *imaginibbles* and advises companies like Proctor & Gamble and IBM on how to foster innovative thinking. When I interviewed her, she shared that getting lots of ideas from different sources is a great way to come up with new ideas for our specific challenges. We're all deep experts in our chosen fields, and Kleinberg suggests dabbling in a lot of areas and taking ideas from those experiences and connecting the dots back to your world.

My lifelong friend Sara White is a marathon runner and

running coach outside her career in educational administration. Through her running, she's traveled the country, served on boards of directors for some of the largest national marathons, coached people of all ages, backgrounds and experience levels, coordinated the logistics for multi-day events, learned about the physiology and psychology of elite running and more. She's also stayed not only sane, but mentally sharp through things like union negotiations, crazy-parent interactions and wholesale technology integrations. She's gotten all of this experience, exposure and learning from her 'hobby'. It's been an edge for her and her career track shows it. She's a better leader and has achieved more because she decided to lace up some running shoes, hit the road and play.

Shall we talk about guilt for a moment? I've had plenty of clients tell me they feel guilty about taking the time, or that it's not fair to their families or company if they're doing something fun or taking time for a hobby. So sorry; I'm not buying it. If you want to spend any time on guilt (which I recommend you give up for the new year if you're still prone to the practice) feel guilty that you're NOT taking time, that you're likely burning yourself out and that you're limiting your opportunities because you are a one-dimensional show.

Get out and play. Get a hobby. Join a team. Be curious

about lots of things and meet new people. You'll be a higher achiever because of it.

Chapter 4 Power Moves

1. Take time off. If you're running the show, set the example by taking ample time off to re-charge your batteries. If you have a certain allotment of vacation days, use every single one of them, every single year.

2. Read a book a year on something totally unrelated to your work. (I had a friend and client who was a Rhodes scholar and now runs a clean energy company who refuses to read anything but fiction. No business, no industry. Subscribe to some interesting magazines (I like National Geographic) and flip through them to learn something new and expand your horizons.

3. Sign up for a course or team through your local community college or city recreation programs. It is unbelievable what's available out there for little to no cost! My daughter and I are going to take a belly dancing class before she leaves for college.

4. Pick one new skill or hobby to take up each year. Next year, I'm going to learn to play the harmonica. I promise

not to do it in public until I'm sure your ears won't bleed if you hear me.

5. Attend a local event like an antique car show, a bike race or gallery opening that you normally wouldn't go to. Make it way outside something you would typically do. Chat some people up. Learn a few things. Enjoy yourself.

Chapter 5 Get Passionate

In 2011 my daughter competed in the Para Pan-American Games in Guadalajara, Mexico. The games were broadcast live on Mexican TV, there was front-page coverage in the newspapers and frequent updates were broadcast on the radio. The Mexican fans sold out the aquatic center every night and their cheers were so loud that I think my ears are still ringing. She rocked the house and brought home both a gold and a silver medal for the United States. Here at home? Not a line, not a word, not a peep in the local media. The national coverage of the games was non-existent. Our local newspaper didn't even run anything.

Here in the USA, we really don't give a damn about our Paralympic athletes, teams or their accomplishments. And you know what? It doesn't matter. That's not what's driving these athletes to compete. They know there are no cars, advertising deals or Wheaties boxes in their future. They compete for the love of their sport, the love of their country and to see what they are personally able to accomplish. I love that champion mindset.

You really have an edge when you work at something you love, for a company or cause you're passionate about, doing your best work. There's been a lot of research and press lately about finding meaning in your work. The ideas aren't new; Abraham Maslow's work just prior to his death was about applying his hierarchy of needs to the business world and finding meaning and purpose through our work. It makes sense. If I'm just showing up at the rock pile every day moving stones, I'll do just that. Show up. When I know those stones are going to go into building a health clinic or research facility, I'll bring my full self to the task. Moving the stones has meaning for me now. I'm doing something constructive. I'm making a difference.

We should all push ourselves to see just how much positive impact we can have. For a long time, I was all about the glory. I wanted to be recognized, in public and preferably with fanfare, for what I brought to the table. Fireworks would have been okay, too. I was chasing the headlines but missing the passion and working hard for all the wrong reasons. It sucked. Yup, I was cranking up the ladder, but the ladder happened to be leaning against the wrong building, and I had put it there. Dissatisfaction and burnout followed.

Super-performers know their own purpose in the world and do work that serves that purpose. They're focused on using their unique talents to make a positive impact. Great leaders make sure that the people they work with understand the larger meaning and purpose in the work they are doing, and you can find this in

ANY industry. For a short while I worked in a division of a printing company that printed phone books. Not sexy. Where was the meaning and purpose in that work? When we connected it to the elderly woman looking up a clinic for her ailing spouse, the meaning started to click. We were printing something that (at that time!) people used to easily find and connect to resources they needed. Suddenly the ink on paper took on a much greater meaning. We were doing something that made a difference.

When you talk with women leading the way, they are all acutely aware of their own purpose and how their work fits into making a difference. They are also givers who share their ideas, serve on non-profit boards and invest in their communities. I have never met a high performer who was not also a generous person.

Now I want to see how much I can do in this world, not because of the accolades but because I want to see how much good I can do. What's possible? I'm no longer looking over my shoulder wondering who is noticing my accomplishments, or striving to achieve some level of success in the hopes of gaining approval from others. Now I aim for an audience of one, internal raving fan who is accomplishing things for love, passion and positive impact.

We have a lot of choices on how we can make money, so go

with something good. I have a great friend whose Dad's advice to him was 'leave things a little better than you found them.' Make sure you're doing the same with your career or business. Make a difference. Do something that will leave positive tracks in the world.

Chapter 5 Power Moves

1. Give. You've got time, talent and treasure at your disposal; give freely of all three.

2. Create a personal, two-word purpose statement. For example, mine is "Fan Flames." My purpose in everything I do is to fan the already burning fire of success, leadership and greatness in women and girls. It took me two years to work this through and really get to the essence of what and why I do what I do, so don't expect to crank this out in a few minutes' time. When you do though, fasten your seatbelt because you're going to be floored by how fast things start moving ahead for you with the clarity and focus a personal purpose statement provides.

3. As a company or department, figure out what the larger meaning in your work is. Why are you doing what you're doing? I recommend watching the TED Talk by Simon Sinek, "Start with Why". You can find it out on YouTube.

Chip Conley wrote a great book, "How Great Companies Get Their Mojo from Maslow" that is also well worth reading as a part of this process.

4. Life's short. Do work you love, or find a way to get meaning from the work you are doing. If you're not loving it, or connected emotionally to the work you're doing in some way, you're not going anywhere big, anytime soon.

5. Before you take on a new project, job or role, check it against your purpose and passion. Can you make a difference? Does it fit in with your 'why'? You're going to be much more successful working on things that have meaning for you than those that don't, so choose wisely.

Conclusion

This book was a little more personal, a little more about who you need to be and how you need to show up to succeed in work and in life. Are you grateful, yet hungry for more? Do you get out and play? Are you treating yourself well? Are you doing meaningful work? Do you believe the world is out to help you? You're probably doing a little in each area and are fantastic in a few. Look through the Power Moves and pick 1-2 that you really think can make a difference and implement them. If you don't already have a purpose statement for yourself, I would really encourage you to start there.

Book five, _5 Habits of Ridiculously Successful Women_, is about the day-to-day and long-term habits that keep you focused and on track in your leadership and achievement pursuit. It's kind of a nuts-and-bolts look at the not very sexy but highly effective habits of achievers.

Email me your gratitude practices, or interesting hobbies or anything else you'd like to share at _Mo@moxieexchange.com_. I'm going to start sharing some insider resources on my blog _www.moxieexchange.com/blog_ and we're really digging in with the Power Moves during the Rock Your Moxie: A Monthly Shot of

163

<u>Leadership & Success</u> workshops – please join us.

Now go out and play for a while!

The 25 Power Moves

Gratitude With a Side of "More"

1. Start a gratitude practice. Every day, name at least 5 things you are grateful for. If you already practice gratitude, up the ante and find a way to include your family, co-workers or close friends in your practice.

2. Share your gratitude freely. "I am so grateful to have you in my life." Or "I am so grateful for the opportunity you gave me." Or "I am so grateful for the x,y,z you bring to the team." Or any version of some genuine statement and sentiment like those is extraordinarily powerful and is a wonderful gift to give the people in your life.

3. Ask people how they express their gratitude at work, and personally. You'll hear all kinds of cool ideas you can adopt for your company or your own gratitude routine.

4. Set your 'more' thermostat to high. Why *not* see how much you can learn and become? Get really comfortable with the idea. After you're comfortable, get really FIRED UP about the idea!

5. Read about some interesting, successful women who fit your definition of 'more'. How did they do it? What are lessons and ideas you can take from their 'more'

excursions?

Assume Good Intentions

1. Start re-training your brain in a hotbed of bad intention thinking: driving in your car. The next time someone cuts you off, or drives 55 in the left-hand lane or swerves into your lane, pay attention to your thinking. Is the script in your head sounding something like, "That friggin' idiot! What in the hell were they thinking?" or other choice phrases? Do a re-frame right then and there. Change your script to something like, "Nobody wants to be in an accident. They must have a boatload going on, or didn't see me. I hope they get to wherever they're going safely." Keep at this exercise until this is your natural first reaction most of the time. There are still going to be the, "You've GOT to be kidding me!" moments, but you'll find they are far and few between, and that your re-framing in the car sets the stage for assuming good intentions everywhere else.

2. Set a goal to notice and acknowledge 3-5 people doing good things in the world each day. When your radar is up for the good stuff, you'll start to see that most people really ARE out to do good versus cause harm.

3. Adopt, "Everyone is doing the best that they can," as a life mantra.

4. When the occasion does arise (and it will) that you come

across someone from 'the dark side' who intentionally hosed you or someone else, respond with empathy. I tend to say something like this to myself, "They must really lead a crappy life to want to do something like that to someone else. I'm glad I'm not living in their world."

5. Remember that we judge ourselves by our intentions and others by their results. When you are questioning why someone did something that outwardly looks like they were up to no good, don't waste energy making up stories about it. You truly have no idea. If you are able, ask them! If you're not, presume their intentions were good, but the results were bad and move on.

Use Premium Fuel

1. Move your body for 30 minutes a day. No excuses. Note that I'm not suggesting you sign up for a premium gym membership, run a marathon or become a black belt. That's not realistic for most people. Just be sure you're physically moving for at least 30 minutes at a stretch. Walk, dance, do a free online yoga class- whatever floats your boat. I take a walk with my husband every day and get the triple bump of time to connect with him, time outdoors and exercise. It is fun to occasionally set a really big stretch goal for yourself on the physical front, too. I've done a few killer trail-running races and ultra team relays

because I wanted to see if I could.

2. Schedule 5 minutes of quiet a day into your schedule. You'll have the best luck doing this consistently if you build it into a routine you already have in place. If you're already doing this, keep rocking it. If not, a good way to start is to simply focus on your breathing- what does it sound like and feel like coming in and out of your body? Unlike full meditation where you are trying to clear your mind, start listening to what thoughts are coming up. Don't judge or sort, just listen and follow it on to the next thought that comes up. You might want to have a pad of paper handy for right after your quiet time to capture some of the ideas that come up for you.

3. Uncover any flawed thinking you may have about your body. I remember it like it was yesterday when my friend Jeff accidentally bumped up against my butt in the 7th grade and said, "It's like Jell-O!" I spent the next 20 years believing my butt was like Jell-O, hating it, and wishing it were small and flat. It wasn't until I started loving and appreciating the body that I do have that I started LOVING having 'junk in the trunk' as we fondly say in my family. I was running the wrong script in my head. Love, appreciate, respect and take care of what you've got, sister. If you need to, get help for any addictions or psychological traumas that are at the root of your beliefs and behaviors. You don't

need to do this solo, and sometimes things are bigger than we can take on ourselves.

4. Adopt a life mantra of "I lead a healthy lifestyle." When you fully embrace this simple but powerful belief, it becomes harder and harder to shove those potato chips in your mouth or have that extra cocktail. Your mind and body start to protect themselves because those behaviors are NOT consistent with your lifestyle.

5. Shop the circumference of the grocery store where the healthy, fresh foods are found. Aim for 'nothing from a can, nothing from a box.'

Get Out and Play

1. Take time off. If you're running the show, set the example by taking ample time off to re-charge your batteries. If you have a certain allotment of vacation days, use every single one of them, every single year.

2. Read a book a year on something totally unrelated to your work. (I had a friend and client who was a Rhodes scholar and now runs a clean energy company who refuses to read anything but fiction. No business, no industry. Subscribe to some interesting magazines (I like National Geographic) and flip through them to learn something new and expand your horizons.

3. Sign up for a course or team through your local community

college or city recreation programs. It is unbelievable what's available out there for little to no cost! My daughter and I are going to take a belly dancing class before she leaves for college.

4. Pick one new skill or hobby to take up each year. Next year, I'm going to learn to play the harmonica. I promise not to do it in public until I'm sure your ears won't bleed if you hear me.

5. Attend a local event like an antique car show, a bike race or gallery opening that you normally wouldn't go to. Make it way outside something you would typically do. Chat some people up. Learn a few things. Enjoy yourself.

Get Passionate

1. Give. You've got time, talent and treasure at your disposal; give freely of all three.

2. Create a personal, two-word purpose statement. For example, mine is "Fan Flames." My purpose in everything I do is to fan the already burning fire of success, leadership and greatness in women and girls. It took me two years to work this through and really get to the essence of what and why I do what I do, so don't expect to crank this out in a few minutes' time. When you do though, fasten your seatbelt because you're going to be floored by how fast things start moving ahead for you with the clarity and

focus a personal purpose statement provides.

3. As a company or department, figure out what the larger meaning in your work is. Why are you doing what you're doing? I recommend watching the TED Talk by Simon Sinek, "Start with Why". You can find it out on YouTube. Chip Conley wrote a great book, "How Great Companies Get Their Mojo from Maslow" that is also well worth reading as a part of this process.

4. Life's short. Do work you love, or find a way to get meaning from the work you are doing. If you're not loving it, or connected emotionally to the work you're doing in some way, you're not going anywhere big, anytime soon.

5. Before you take on a new project, job or role, check it against your purpose and passion. Can you make a difference? Does it fit in with your 'why'? You're going to be much more successful working on things that have meaning for you than those that don't, so choose wisely.

Rock your *Moxie*

Power Moves for Women Leading the Way

5 **Habits** *of* Ridiculously Successful Women

by Maureen Berkner Boyt

Rock Your Moxie:

Power Moves for Women Leading the Way

5 Habits of Ridiculously Successful Women

Maureen Berkner Boyt

Table of Contents

Click here to join a community of women in an online monthly workshop covering ideas and Power Moves from the book

Chapter 1 Lay a Killer Foundation

"It takes as much energy to wish as it does to plan" - Eleanor Roosevelt. Eleanor is one of my heroines, and that quote is one of my favorites of all time. With those 12 words, she captures the essence of why some women are uber-successful and most seem stuck in the mud, grinding out their forward progress. There are a whole lot of women with big dreams and no plans for making them happen. Those women who are moving and shaking are fantastic at planning and brilliant at executing on those plans. It all starts with setting yourself up for success at the start of the year and laying a killer foundation for success.

I can ask women one simple question and fairly accurately chart their levels of leadership and success for the next few years. The question is, *"What are your top five goals for the coming year?"* Typical responses include some vague numbers about sales growth or getting a new job, wanting to spend some more time with the family, lose a little weight, maybe take a vacation. For really successful women though, it's a little like asking five-year-olds to show you their favorite toys. They get really excited and animated and their energy shoots through the roof. They'll always start to paint a very clear picture of what they are out to achieve in the year. I had one woman hop up and literally pull me into her conference room to show me the goals she's had *painted* on the walls there. Frequently smart phones will be whipped out or well-worn pieces of paper emerge from bags so these women can tell me about their plans and show me at the same time.

Really successful women are addicted to good planning. They've got a 'planning' habit!

If you've never been a planner, or fall into the New Year's Eve resolution crowd, it's time to get over that. Otherwise, you're going to be sitting in about the same place next year that you are right now. I'm guessing you're at least a good planner or you wouldn't be reading book five in this series. The majority of people are stumbling around with what amounts to a blindfold on. They have no idea where they are headed in life and in business. Many women spend more time finding a great pair of jeans or that killer bag or screwing around on Pinterest than they do thinking about and planning out their future. That seriously bums me out. What an enormous waste of potential and talent! What that means for you, though, is that the more you plan and work those plans, the further and more quickly the gap between you and average widens.

I want you to be a rock star, gold-standard planner. I want you to plan like the top 10% do, and there are a few key steps in that process. It starts with creating a solid foundation by knowing where you're heading in the long term, how things stack up for you right now, what's driving your current success and what you're aiming for in the current year. Let's take those one at a time.

No matter what time of year you are reading this book, I want you to start your planning process by getting very, very clear about where you are headed. That starts with writing a letter to yourself as if it is four to five years in the future and you are leading your ideal life. Start with, "It's 20XX, and I am 'x' years old." Then in detail, write what your life is like. Include relationships, what you're doing professionally and your work accomplishments, how much money you are making, what your spiritual life is like, what kind of house you're living in, what hobbies you're spending time on, where you are traveling… you get my drift. Take your time! The first time I wrote this type of letter to myself, it took me two weeks to complete it. I left it sitting out so when some new idea occurred to me, I could quickly find my letter and add it to the mix. Remember, this is your dream; make it GOOD! Set your 'deserve' thermostat to HIGH and start writing. When your letter is complete, you will have created a long-term target and goals for your life.

After you're clear about where you're headed, it's time to

take stock of your personal and leadership habits to see if they are serving you or hindering you. Humans are routine-based creatures and we do most things out of habit. Taking stock is about analyzing whether your habits, professional and personal, are healthy or destructive. Our choices are either helping or hurting us; there is no neutral. Leave no stone unturned. Look at your habits and choices in areas like friends, diet, mental diet, amount of time on email, sleep, money and financials, social media, alcohol, delegation, sex, team communication, exercise and the like. Be very, very honest with yourself. What habits are serving you and which are holding you back? If you don't like something, change it! Remember to fail forward and know you're going to stumble and fall back into some bad habits. The brilliant thing is, when you do, you can choose again! If I slip up and jack back a bag of Fritos, I can choose again to lead a healthy lifestyle. If I micromanage my team, I can choose again to be a great delegator. We have the power to keep choosing habits that are serving us.

The next step is to seek feedback and analyze how the past year went professionally. Which way did things break for you - up or down? Have you figured out why, and have you stopped the things that held you back and increased the things that powered you forward? You're going to need to ask people who have worked with you for their input on your performance, and answer the questions for yourself as well. Dig in to things like: What strengths do you need to leverage? What opportunities do you need to pursue? What should you hold off on? What are your go/no-go criteria for pursuing new opportunities? What are your unique strengths? What skills do you need to bone up on to be ready for the next role or challenge you've set your sights on? Where did I 'fail' and what did I learn? This is a great time to seek the input of the mentors and sponsors in your life, too. They are going to have a unique perspective on both you and what you need to do to prepare for what's next for you.

Now that you know where you are headed, you've tweaked your personal and professional habits so they support your success, you're clear on your leadership and professional skills and behaviors and clear on what you need to do more of, less of and learn, it is time to create your one-year success plan. We overcomplicate the hell out of these, and some consulting firms and coaches want you to believe there is voodoo involved. Not so. Read over the work you have done. Take a hard look at your ideal life in 4-5 years and ask yourself this question, "What are the five things I need to accomplish *this year*, to hit my four-to five-year goals?"

Start writing. Ideas should be coming to you pretty quickly because you'll have seen themes emerging from the work you've already done. Review your ideas. Refine, tweak, group together and combine. Set it aside. Come back in a few hours or a day and review again. When you have your *Big 5* for the year, have someone who knows what you're out to accomplish read them. Tweak based on their feedback. When you really feel like you've nailed them and you have THE five key goals that are going to drive your success, celebrate. You just laid a killer foundation to kick butt and take names in the coming year.

Chapter 1 Power Moves

1. Pull out your calendar and schedule your planning and review sessions for the coming year. Block out at least a day to plan and prepare your annual plan, four hours per quarter for a quarterly review, 1 hour per month for monthly planning, 15 minutes per week for weekly planning and 10 minutes a day for daily priority setting. If you are not willing to do this, you might want to consider not reading the rest of the book. Success is about having a solid plan and executing on those plans, and that won't happen if you don't prioritize the time. Wishing won't get you there.

2. Write a letter to yourself in the future, making it at least 4 years out. Have your spouse or partner do the same thing, and compare letters. Doing this exercise was one of the

accelerators of my success, and really enhanced my relationship with my husband. We were already happy, but this really got us in lockstep about what we wanted in our lives.

3. Take stock of your habits. Don't sugar coat. If you can't be honest with yourself, you're not going to make the necessary changes. Listen to the little voice that's telling you something needs to change; she's trying to help.

4. Seek feedback from your team. What do they need from you to be dynamite? What do they believe you should work on to be a better leader? What do they believe you should leverage to really rock the house? Get your mentors and sponsors to share their feedback with you about what you need to learn and how you need to prepare for what's next.

5. Set aside a day for planning and go somewhere that is relaxing and inspiring for you. I've done this on a mountainside, in a museum coffee shop, in a park and in a room at a funky boutique hotel. Create your annual plan, with no more than five major goals or initiatives for the year. Some are going to be professional, some are going to be personal. If you have more than five, they're either too

small and shouldn't make your top 5 list, or you have too many and they are not going to happen. When you're done, do a small happy dance or perhaps shout out a big, "Whoop! Whoop!"

Chapter 2 Check the Stars

Wouldn't it be slick if things worked out the way we planned, with no changes or surprises? More often, we have the, "Well I never saw THAT one coming!" type experiences, bad or good. This last year alone I had clients who were surprised by: an unexpected pregnancy at 45, a major client taking their work in-house, costing the company 35% of its revenues overnight, a cancer diagnosis, a business partner changing their mind mid-buyout, a board recommendation for the CEO position. None of them saw it coming, and ALL of them were able to roll with the punches and integrate the unexpected into their plans for themselves.

If you re-read that list, those were some pretty big surprises. Why did they take them in stride? Because planning is not an annual 'event' for highly successful women; *they have a habit of checking their progress and adjusting their plans throughout the year.*

The women who were thrown the 180s were able to move ahead because they took the new information and circumstances and integrated them into their quarterly plans. I call this process 'checking the stars', much like sailors and pilots did long ago to make sure they were staying on course. Nailing your annual growth plan is the start to the process. But conducting quarterly check-ins and making adjustments based on your assessments, new information and current circumstances is where things really get rolling.

Start the process immediately following the creation of your annual plan. You need to chunk down your annual plan into four smaller quarterly plans with specific goals and initiatives for each quarter. A few things are going to be time-sensitive, and you can load those into your plan for the year. For example if there's a course you plan on taking or industry-driven deadlines, make sure you've got those in the associated quarterly plan.

Mostly, though, you'll be coming up with the majority of your quarterly goals about two weeks before the start of a quarter. Take half a day and review what occurred in the last quarter. How are my assumptions playing out? What's going well? Are there any resources I need to help drive forward? Have I gotten any feedback about my performance or the market that I need to integrate into this quarter's plan? What have I learned? Am I taking enough risk? Are there any challenges or struggles I am facing? Again, I would suggest seeking feedback from the people around you. Making decisions based solely on your own thinking might be faster in the short term, but is rarely a good idea down the road! Once you have a good sense about where things stand, set your plans for the upcoming quarter.

Do this just as you did when you looked at your long-term goals and determined your annual plan. Ask yourself, "What needs to happen *this* quarter in order for me to achieve my Big 5 annual goals?" Do a "brain dump" as the ideas are coming, go through the refinement process and come up with your *Top 5* goals that you're going to focus your time and energy on over the next 90 days.

At this point, it's also important to take some time and acknowledge and celebrate what went right in the past quarter. What were your 'wins'? Did you have any major breakthroughs or interesting ah-has? You worked hard, so pause for a moment and let that soak in; then do something cool for yourself!

Consider shining a spotlight on one or two of your goals in a quarter and do a Full-On 45. For 45 days straight, no breaks for holidays or weekends, do at least one thing to move you forward on a specific goal. I love visual tracking (the star charts in 1st grade made me swoon!) so I usually create a quick spreadsheet that I'll print out and stick up on my wall. Each day in the Full-On 45, your goal is to have a checkmark in the box indicating you've gotten something done toward your goal. I've been known to blast out an email or do a set of push-ups late in the evening because, come hell or high water, I was going to get that box checked! And that's the point of the Full-On 45; it induces activity and in turn results.

Chapter 2 Power Moves

1. Step out of your day-to-day for four hours and have a mini planning retreat. Gather any information you might need in advance so you can truly 'get away' for those few hours. Turn off your phone, shut down your computer and get in a planning state of mind!

2. Review the previous quarter: wins, learning, challenges, assumptions, feedback. Really kick around what happened and assess where things stand.

3. Set your Top Five for the quarter. Make sure they are the most important things you should be focused on to help you achieve your annual goals.

4. If you don't have one or don't participate in one, consider getting an accountability partner or executive coach or joining a mastermind group. Pick someone, or a group you know and respect, who is out to succeed in big ways like you are. The people you select are invaluable resources in

helping you to see flaws or gaps in your plan, bringing new thinking and ideas to the party, and keeping you moving in the right direction toward next-level achievement. Every successful woman I know has an accountability partner, a coach, a mastermind group or all three that she works with.

5. Choose an area of focus and complete a Full-On 45. Not only is it a good challenge, you'll find it a bit addicting because of the progress and results you'll achieve.

Chapter 3 Wiggle A Little

One of the key things we've built into the Moxie Exchange Movement's meeting process is something we call Power Planning; we also affectionately refer to it as "the gift of time." Every month, like clockwork, Moxie members pull out a Power Planning worksheet and rewrite their Big Five for the year and set five personal and five professional goals for the month that are going to help them achieve their Big Five. I get stories about how the worksheets are used that range from, 'It's wadded up on the floorboard of my car, so I see it every time I drive somewhere', to 'I turn my monthly priorities into a screen saver so they are always in front of me.' I ran into one of the members at the grocery store this summer and she laughingly pulled her worksheet out of her bag and said, "Staying on track!" What we consistently hear, and what the research supports, is that the simple act of rewriting big goals and getting clarity around the key priorities for the month has a positive impact on making those goals happen.

It was non-negotiable in my mind when I was designing the Moxie meeting structure that goal setting be a part of the meeting process. I wanted to bake in the habit wickedly successful women have of *rewriting and chunking down their big goals into manageable, actionable plans.*

This is where solid planning starts to take a turn toward brilliant execution. On a monthly basis, carve out an hour to rewrite your Big 5 for the year. It's important to rewrite or type them, not just think about them. Depending on the research you read, your chances of attaining your goals rise as much as 35% to 70% from that act alone. Review your quarterly Top 5, and you get a gold star in my book if you re-write them as well. Then think about the month ahead. Are there any time-bound things like reporting or reviews that need to take place? Make sure they

make it into your monthly priorities. How is the progress toward your plans shaping up? Do you need to make any small adjustments based on what you're learning and accomplishing? I do mean small, not, "I'm throwing in the towel or lowering the bar because this is hard." The adjustments should be more like wiggling the handle on a door so the lock will click into place. Finally, ask yourself, "What are the five things I need to accomplish *this* month to achieve my quarterly Top 5?" Write 'em down! You now have your Monthly 5.

I'm sure you're starting to see the pattern and rhythm in this process so there won't be much shock about the next steps. Every Sunday evening or Monday morning, review and re-write your Monthly 5 and your previous Weekly Top 5. Look at the week ahead and determine what five things you need to accomplish *this* week to nail those objectives for the month. Put your Weekly Top 5 in writing in a really accessible place because you'll be reviewing them every, single day.

I cannot stress enough how critical this activity is to your on-going, forward progress. I also know how very, very easy it is to blow it off and head into your week with no plan. Most people do, but not you! Those 15 minutes set you up to have a spectacular week. On the rare occasion that I don't do this planning, my week really stinks; I get blown by the winds of other people's priorities and waste time like it's nobody's business. Weekly planning and priority setting is one of the highest impact success activities there is, and it only takes 15 measly minutes!

Chapter 3 Power Moves

1. Schedule one hour per month to rewrite your Big 5, review your Top 5 and determine your Monthly 5.

2. DO THE PLANNING! Scheduling the time is easy, actually creating the plan is where most people slip up. Wiggle and adjust a little so your Monthly 5 are relevant, and take into account the progress and new learning that has taken place the month prior.

192

3. Schedule 15 minutes on Sunday evening or Monday morning to get clear on how you are going to kick *ss, take names and be absurdly productive in the coming week.

4. Design a planning worksheet for yourself that captures your annual, quarterly and monthly plans. I'm happy to send you mine, just email me at mo@moxieexchange.com and I'll send you a copy.

5. Get some sort of 'keeper of your priorities'. It may be something technology based like Evernote, or a simple 3-ring notebook. I'm addicted to Moleskine notebooks, and I capture all of my Weekly Top 5 plans in one of them.

Chapter 4 One Small Bag

For the last four months, all of my belongings have fit into one small bag. We packed up our house and have been on a family adventure living abroad, so everything I have I can carry around on my back in a small backpack. For a few legs of our journey, our bags needed to weigh 22 pounds or less, so we could fly places for ridiculously cheap on Ryanair. When you get used to being hyper critical about what makes it into the bag, the choosing gets pretty easy. Creativity begins to kick in, too. Those weeks of 22 pounds? After my laptop and the weight of the bag itself, I had a whopping 12 pounds to play with. No to jewelry. No to the cute scarf. Wear the heavy stuff, tote the light stuff.

Hot damn is it a freeing feeling! The weight of 'stuff' is off my shoulders. All I need to keep track of fits in one small space. The items are vital and manageable at the same time. Of course, being the leadership and success geek that I am, the analogy of the 'one small bag' rule and setting daily priorities makes perfect sense. They are both about getting down to the essentials and weeding out the should do's from the must do's, the want to do's from the need to do's. Using the O.S.B. rule, the list gets pretty short every day. It gets down to crucial and manageable.

A habit of highly successful women is planning their days down to the nitty-gritty, and working on the high-value, high-impact priorities first.

Now we're really talking about what separates women at the top and average players. If you really want 'more,' you have to get good at fundamental, daily execution on the things that move you and your plans forward. You have a finite amount of time in each day, and if you want to nail your goals and live your 'ideal' life' scenario, you've got to get damned good at working on the right things, consistently, day in and day out. This is not sexy, or shiny or new-fangled. You have heard this before. And for most people, the knowing/doing gap persists. In all my interactions with successful women, there is a theme of showing up, every day, consistently over time and working on the right things. Estee Lauder said it well, "When I thought I couldn't go on, I forced myself to keep going. My success is based on persistence, not luck."

We are never going to get the time we spend today back. It is precious and it is so, so easy to piss away. Just one more episode of "x", just one more time hitting the snooze button, just one more... It took me a long time to realize that *discipline equals freedom*. The more disciplined I am about working on my daily top priorities, the more freedom it allows me to choose how I spend my time in the long run.

That starts with setting daily priorities that feed long range plans. It means really getting into the details of each day. It's really fun to dream and make big plans. Your plans aren't worth the paper they're written on though if you are not making them come to life each day by executing on them in small, forward progress bites. We need to think about our daily priorities as focusing on the fundamentals and essentials of our success. Setting and executing on a daily plan takes a small amount of time, but is crucially important to us becoming 'more'.

How do you determine what should make it into your one, small bag each day? Focus on what your goals are for the week. Your daily priorities become the 5 things you need to do TODAY to make them happen.

Block out the morning hours in your calendar every day to work on your priorities. No excuses. There will always be 'stuff' that needs to be done. Do it later. It will be waiting for you. There will always be someone who wants to meet with you. Suggest a time that works in your schedule *after* you have worked on your priorities. You'll be amazed at how flexible people are regarding when they can meet, if only we ASK. They've typically just thrown out a time with not a lot of attachment to when a meeting actually takes place. Make it work in your calendar. If you're not in control of your meeting schedule, adjust your daily planning practice to include blocking in time around your fixed schedule for the day. You have to set an appointment for yourself to work on your priorities, or I guarantee the time will get sucked up by something non-essential. There's always going to be another email to check, or co-worker to discuss a project with. You need to be lioness-protective of your daily plan execution time.

Chapter 4 Power Moves

1. Block chunks of time in your calendar marked as "daily plan execution" or "Top 5," indicating when you will be executing on your daily priorities.

2. Review your plans for the week and what you accomplished the prior day; then set your Top 5 for the day. Write them down! I'm old school in this regard because I like having a small notebook I keep track of my priorities in. Use whatever tool works best for you, but make sure they are written and accessible to you throughout the day.

3. Check in on your progress against your list late-morning. What have you accomplished? Make schedule adjustments as needed.

4. Track those daily priorities that somehow always seem to fall to the bottom of the list and not get done. You probably have some kind of fear around it. Figure out what it is, name it and START with that priority the following morning. If it's simply a matter of you not liking it, suck it up, cupcake! That monkey on your back is NOT an attractive accessory.

5. At the end of the day, check your progress. Transfer anything that didn't get done to tomorrow's list, and check things off that you've completed. Again, I'm all about the small, visual rewards of check marks and the like, and I have an orange pen I cross things off my list with. I add a little mental flair to the process, too, often thinking things like, "Yeah, baby! Slayed THAT dragon today!" Do whatever motivates you to keep working on your daily priorities, day in and day out. It's *the* habit of the successful.

Chapter 5 Use The Secret Sauce

It's time for the secret sauce habit. Really, it's a cluster of smaller habits done at a specific time each day.

There are two magic windows of time in every 24 hours that power women utilize to their fullest. Most of our days are hectic, packed and happen to involve a LOT of other people. As soon as other people's priorities and requests start to butt up against our own, we've got to be nimble on our feet and really flexible to stay connected to, and working on, *our* priorities. The demands on our time and energy start almost right out of the gates. Especially if you have kids at home, the morning-rush-out-the-door-to-school can be a little like being hit by a small Tsunami each morning.

Successful women habitually utilize the first and last 30-60 minutes of their day as a power hour.

Think about how you typically start your day. If you are like most, you either roll over, grab your phone and check to see if you have any new emails or texts, or fire up your laptop and log into a social media site. In that one small act, you have just given up control of your day. You have not even gotten out of bed, and you've allowed someone else to start pulling your puppet strings. They are making you dance to the tune of their priorities, or worse yet, hypnotizing you with photos of what they had for dinner last night. Not good. If you keep your cell phone or laptop in your bedroom, get the damned thing out of there right now!

It's time for a new set of morning habits that set you up for a rock star day. Women I work with have their own combo of the things I'm going to share, so make this recipe your own. Here are some morning habits I know high-performing women consistently begin their days with. 1) Start with gratitude. Spend a quiet few minutes thinking about or writing down the things you are grateful for in your life. 2) Get some exercise like a quick walk or run, or yoga. 3) Read something that feeds your brain. It can be something inspiring or something that drives learning on a topic you are interested in. 4) Re-write your Big 5, and set your Daily Top 5 priorities with time blocks 5) Dream. Spend a few minutes dreaming about where you are headed and create in your mind how your ideal day is going to go. After you've done one to two of these, it's safe to check your email. You've got your head on straight and are focused on your success and priorities, and you will be far less likely to take the bait on fighting someone else's fire.

Yes, you do have the time for this. Set your alarm 30 minutes earlier than you normally do or than the rest of the family wakes up. You will be *stunned* how much you're going to get done in those 30 minutes and how it shapes your day in a positive way.

How are you ending your day? The National Sleep Foundation's poll revealed that 95% of people frequently used some form of technology, from TV to texting, before bed, so I feel pretty safe in guessing how you're wrapping things up. Now that you've booted the cell phones and laptops out of your bedroom, adopt a few of these common bedtime habits of successful women. 1) Review your day. Think about things that made you feel successful and what you learned during the day. 2) Set your Daily Top 5 for the following day. 3) Write a thank you note. 4) Read something that feeds your brain. It can be something inspiring or something that drives learning on a topic you are interested in. 5) Get quiet and listen to your thoughts.

Yes, you do have the time for this. Go to bed 20 minutes earlier than you normally do.

Think of the start and end of your day as a secret sauce for bringing together all your leadership and achievement beliefs, behaviors and habits. They are a magic time for you to renew and refresh so you are engaged and energized to start each day as an achiever.

Chapter 5 Power Moves

1. Get your cell phone and laptop out of your bedroom. No excuses.

2. Set your alarm for 30 minutes earlier than you normally do. NEVER use a snooze button. Do you really want to start your day by procrastinating? Not a good habit!

3. Pick a few of the morning habits and routines I outlined and try them on for size. I really encourage you to build some form of exercise or physical activity into your morning routine. The research on how it fires up your brain and increases your energy levels is conclusive.

4. Pick a few of the bedtime habits and routines I outlined and see which ones really work for you. Turn off the TV at least 45 minutes before you plan on hitting the sack.

5. Get quiet and listen to your thoughts.

Conclusion

Discipline equals freedom. If you choose to improve your planning and execution habits, you will get farther ahead, faster. You will achieve more and become more than 95% of the population. You'll be grabbing the reigns on the next leadership and growth opportunity in short order. Dream, plan, assess your progress, chunk it down, get gritty, do. Repeat. Period and end of book and *Rock Your Moxie* series.

Actually, not quite. I want to acknowledge what a rock star you are. You are a growth-oriented, get-it-done, lead-the-way kind of woman. I really, really hope we get to meet one day; I love hanging out with women like you! You are a part of my community and I wrote these books for you. I'd love it if you weren't a stranger and added your voice to the other women out for 'more'. Join in the conversation and share your leadership journey as a member of the <u>Rock Your Moxie: A Monthly Shot of Leadership & Success</u> tribe or email <u>mo@moxieexchange.com</u>

I also want you to think about the girls in your life, be they daughters, nieces, or neighbors. They are watching you. They are watching us as women in the power arena of business. They see when we acknowledge our strengths and own our brilliance. They observe us asking for more. They believe they can lead when they see us leading. Let's show them what we've got, shall we?

Rock your moxie!

The 25 Power Moves

Lay A Killer Foundation

1. Pull out your calendar and schedule your planning and review sessions for the coming year. Block out at least a day to plan and prepare your annual plan, four hours per quarter for a quarterly review, 1 hour per month for monthly planning, 15 minutes per week for weekly planning and 10 minutes a day for daily priority setting. If you are not willing to do this, you might want to consider not reading the rest of the book. Success is about having a solid plan and executing on those plans, and that won't happen if you don't prioritize the time. Wishing won't get you there.

2. Write a letter to yourself in the future, making it at least 4 years out. Have your spouse or partner do the same thing, and compare letters. Doing this exercise was one of the accelerators of my success, and really enhanced my relationship with my husband. We were already happy, but this really got us in lockstep about what we wanted in our lives.

3. Take stock of your habits. Don't sugar coat. If you can't be honest with yourself, you're not going to make the

necessary changes. Listen to the little voice that's telling you something needs to change; she's trying to help.

4. Seek feedback from your team. What do they need from you to be dynamite? What do they believe you should work on to be a better leader? What do they believe you should leverage to really rock the house? Get your mentors and sponsors to share their feedback with you about what you need to learn and how you need to prepare for what's next.

5. Set aside a day for planning and go somewhere that is relaxing and inspiring for you. I've done this on a mountainside, in a museum coffee shop, in a park and in a room at a funky boutique hotel. Create your annual plan, with no more than five major goals or initiatives for the year. Some are going to be professional, some are going to be personal. If you have more than five, they're either too small and shouldn't make your top 5 list, or you have too many and they are not going to happen. When you're done, do a small happy dance or perhaps shout out a big, "Whoop! Whoop!"

Check the Stars

1. Step out of your day-to-day for four hours and have a mini planning retreat. Gather any information you might need

in advance so you can truly 'get away' for those few hours. Turn off your phone, shut down your computer and get in a planning state of mind

2. Review the previous quarter: wins, learning, challenges, assumptions, feedback. Really kick around what happened and assess where things stand.

3. Set your Top Five for the quarter. Make sure they are the most important things you should be focused on to help you achieve your annual goals.

4. If you don't have one or don't participate in one, consider getting an accountability partner or executive coach or joining a mastermind group. Pick someone, or a group you know and respect, who is out to succeed in big ways like you are. The people you select are invaluable resources in helping you to see flaws or gaps in your plan, bringing new thinking and ideas to the party, and keeping you moving in the right direction toward next-level achievement. Every successful woman I know has an accountability partner, a coach, a mastermind group or all three that she works with.

5. Choose an area of focus and complete a Full-On 45. Not only is it a good challenge, you'll find it a bit addicting because of the progress and results you'll achieve.

Wiggle A Little

1. Schedule one hour per month to rewrite your Big 5, review your Top 5 and determine your Monthly 5.

2. DO THE PLANNING! Scheduling the time is easy, actually creating the plan is where most people slip up. Wiggle and adjust a little so your Monthly 5 are relevant, and take into account the progress and new learning that has taken place the month prior.

3. Schedule 15 minutes on Sunday evening or Monday morning to get clear on how you are going to kick *ss, take names and be absurdly productive in the coming week.

4. Design a planning worksheet for yourself that captures your annual, quarterly and monthly plans. I'm happy to send you mine, just email me at mo@moxieexchange.com and I'll send you a copy.

5. Get some sort of 'keeper of your priorities'. It may be something technology based like Evernote, or a simple 3-ring notebook. I'm addicted to Moleskine notebooks, and I capture all of my Weekly Top 5 plans in one of them.

One Small Bag

1. Block chunks of time in your calendar marked as "daily plan execution" or "Top 5," indicating when you will be executing on your daily priorities.

2. Review your plans for the week and what you

accomplished the prior day; then set your Top 5 for the day. Write them down! I'm old school in this regard because I like having a small notebook I keep track of my priorities in. Use whatever tool works best for you, but make sure they are written and accessible to you throughout the day.

3. Check in on your progress against your list late-morning. What have you accomplished? Make schedule adjustments as needed.

4. Track those daily priorities that somehow always seem to fall to the bottom of the list and not get done. You probably have some kind of fear around it. Figure out what it is, name it and START with that priority the following morning. If it's simply a matter of you not liking it, suck it up, cupcake! That monkey on your back is NOT an attractive accessory.

5. At the end of the day, check your progress. Transfer anything that didn't get done to tomorrow's list, and check things off that you've completed. Again, I'm all about the small, visual rewards of check marks and the like, and I have an orange pen I cross things off my list with. I add a little mental flair to the process, too, often thinking things like, "Yeah, baby! Slayed THAT dragon today!" Do whatever motivates you to keep working on your daily priorities, day in and day out. It's *the* habit of the

successful.

Use the Secret Sauce

1. Get your cell phone and laptop out of your bedroom. No excuses.
2. Set your alarm for 30 minutes earlier than you normally do. NEVER use a snooze button. Do you really want to start your day by procrastinating? Not a good habit!
3. Pick a few of the morning habits and routines I outlined and try them on for size. I really encourage you to build some form of exercise or physical activity into your morning routine. The research on how it fires up your brain and increases your energy levels is conclusive.
4. Pick a few of the bedtime habits and routines I outlined and see which ones really work for you. Turn off the TV at least 45 minutes before you plan on hitting the sack.
5. Get quiet and listen to your thoughts.

Author Biography

Maureen Berkner Boyt is the Founder of The Moxie Exchange Movement and its girl's leadership development program, The Go Girl Project. She is a thought partner to organizations and women serious about leadership development and learning. She holds a M.Ed. in Organizational Development, is a graduate of Corporate Coach U, and is a life-long student of leadership, business and success. She has coached over 100 leaders, founded multiple successful businesses, lived and worked internationally, and loves taking business ideas and making them come to life.

Maureen knows that every woman is capable of being an extraordinary leader and of achieving ridiculous levels of success in their lives. Her passion is bringing out the potential in female leaders and she truly believes that when women are fully represented at the executive levels in business, we will begin to solve large global problems in a meaningful way. Maureen also believes that we need to tuck the next generation of female leaders under our wings when they are still girls so that they can step into their leadership at an earlier age.

She'd love to connect with you on her blog www.moxieexchange.com/blog www.moxieexchange.com/blog, by email mo@moxieexchange.com, as a part of the Rock Your Moxie: A Monthly Shot of Leadership & Success community or on LinkedIn where she can cryptically be found by typing in her name.

In the **Rock Your Moxie** series, Maureen Berkner Boyt shares personal stories and insights from her years of interviewing and interacting with women who are at the top of their game, yet still want more. Each chapter concludes with key Power Moves that are an *achievement-inducing roadmap* for you to up your leadership game and claim your seat at the table. If you are ready to think and act your way into your *next level of success,* this series was written just for you.

Includes 125 Power Moves!

Maureen Berkner Boyt is the Founder and President of The Moxie Exchange Movement, a thriving community of women and organizations committed to women's leadership development and success. She has worked with thousands of women around the world and is a popular keynote speaker and executive coach. She lives in Fort Collins, Colorado with her husband and two children.

43868622R00121

Made in the USA
San Bernardino, CA
30 December 2016